SELF-HELP
FOR THE
BLEAK

SELF-HELP
FOR THE
BLEAK

RICH HALL
EDITED BY ANN SLICHTER

PRICE STERN SLOAN, INC.
A MEMBER OF
THE PUTNAM BERKLEY GROUP, INC.
NEW YORK

Published by Price Stern Sloan, Inc.
a member of
The Putnam Berkley Group, Inc.
200 Madison Avenue
New York, NY 10016

Grateful acknowledgment is made for permission to reprint excerpts from the following:

(p. 35) Portions of the lyric from "Buffalo River Home," by John Hiatt © 1993 Careers-BMG Music Publishing, Inc. (BMI) and Whistling Moon Traveler Music (BMI). All rights reserved. Used by permission.

Library of Congress Cataloging-in-Publication Data

Hall, Rich, date.
    Self-help for the bleak / by Rich Hall.
       p. cm.
    ISBN 0-8431-3669-3
     1. Life—Humor.   2. Self-actualization (Psychology)—Humor.
I. Title.
   PN6231.L48H35   1994
   818'.5402—dc20   93-13615   CIP

Printed in the United States of America
3   4   5   6   7   8   9   10

This book is printed on acid-free paper.

Dedication

To the wonderful people of Deadrock, every one of them.

Acknowledgments

The following people really helped:

Tom Hertz (who gave me his great tollbooth idea), Leonard & Larry, Tracy Abbott, Tim Kelleher, Mimi Kiser, Rick Overton, Jeff Cesario, Bob Lovka, Sheena Needham, Laura Bellotti, Larry the Whispering Indian, Katherine Johnson (especially), somebody at Federal Express, Dave Becky, Mike Connors, Ralph Bronner, Digby Diehl, Daniel, Joel Hodgson, the Jazz Butcher (who is playing right now as I type) and most importantly of all, my indispensable editor, Ann Slichter!

Contents

INTRODUCTION

No one influenced me more than Dr. Norman Vincent Peale. I never thought I'd get to meet him and when I did, he was quite old and feeble. But there was steel in his eyes and firmness in his grip, and I remember thinking, "This isn't the guy I meant. I meant Dale Carnegie."

—R.H.

I think the lowest point in my life was when my company, House of Index Cards, Inc., fish bellied. I suppose I dealt with it the way most people would, turning the blame inward. I told myself I was an idiot for ever thinking a chain of mall-based index card emporiums would catch on. I told myself I didn't have a head for business. And then I let myself get depressed. I remember sitting in a storage unit full of 22,000 cartons of unsold index cards thinking, "What's the point of going on with my life?"

There was a shrinkwrap machine in the corner, a huge pneumatic spindle for bundling index cards. It would have been so sweet and painless to climb on, flip a switch and spin myself into a prepackaged eternal slumber. The machine could even label me: BIG FAT ZERO.

The only thing that kept me hanging in there was my girlfriend. One evening I was home listening to a "How To Declare Chapter 11" motivational tape when she came in distraught and shaking. She'd had a blowout on the turnpike and almost skidded into a ravine—a near-death experience.

Well sir, because I was concerned for her personal safety and because it was her birthday, I took her out and bought her a brand new set of all-weather radials. She never mounted those tires. In fact, they sat untouched in my garage. Maybe she thought they were too sentimental to ruin on asphalt.

Later, after she dumped me, I would go out to the garage and sit and try to figure out why everything I touched turned to shit. Here I was bankrupt, my girlfriend was history, and I was broke, lonely, dispirited and bleak. I couldn't even call up my Aunt Gretel for consolation because somebody at the Harriet Tubman Women's Shelter was hogging the pay phone.

Staring at those four, sturdy well-balanced tires made me envious. Why wasn't my life riding on four good tires? See, I have this theory that our lives rest on four essential Tires: a Love Tire, a Mental-Physical Health Tire, a Career Tire and a Spiritual Tire.

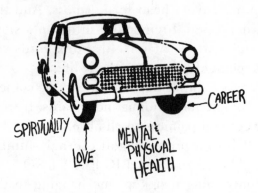

Go ahead and laugh, but I've seen entire self-help movements based on flimsier premises!

See, when it comes to the Four Tires of Living, very few of us are actually driving a balanced vehicle. Rather, our lives quite often resemble the fellow below:

THE CLASSIC WORKAHOLIC

That was me behind that wheel! The only thing that mattered was getting my Index Card business off the ground. I thought if my Career Tire was big enough, it would just crush all the competition. Did I pay any attention to my other tires? The Spirituality Tire? Hardly. Mental-Physical Health Tire? No, sir. The Love Tire? Hey, ask my ex-girlfriend. All she ever heard was the blub-blub-blub-blub of one Flat Love Tire caressing every pothole in the road. And that's why she dumped me.

I was a workaholic! I was driving on one big fat over-inflated Career Tire like some mutant Big Daddy Garlits Off-Road funny car, and when it blew, brother, I realized I had been going nowhere but in circles.

That night in the garage a powerful idea came to me. Why not recycle my mistakes into a book that might help others? (There's a reason they're called self-help books: I could make millions.) So that's what I'm doing. I'm writing a book that can help you get your life balanced on four solid tires. And ever since I've begun writing, nothing—absolutely nothing else—matters. I'm *committed*, brother.

Why I'm Uniquely Qualified to Write This Book

A quick bit of background on myself and then we'll get to the meat and gristle of the book. Although I have had modest success as an entertainer, I consider my 4 Tires of Living lecture seminars to be my crowning work. A visible figure on both the Rotary and Kiwanis circuits, as well as at dozens of community colleges and vocational-technical institutes, I have guested some of the finest pancake breakfasts, multi-purpose rooms and cafeteria "nooners" in the country.

Invariably, audiences ask what qualifies me to be a lecturer. I always answer with one word: "Failure!"

Successful people have little to teach us. We learn from *mistakes*. And, friend, I have a Ph.D. in mistakes.

How I crawled back from that sucking vortex of hopelessness and despair and regained my self-esteem would certainly make an inspiring novel, particularly for youngsters aged 8 to 13. But I have chosen to forego the inspirational route (and imminent Caldecott medal) for a more practical step-by-step guide to putting your life back together. Read on, my friend, and let me spin my straw mistakes into golden advice.

YOUR LOVE TIRE

"aaaaaaaaaagh!"

—Morrissey

A Word About Your Love Tire

As a tire, Love gets abused beyond belief: wildly overinflated, then allowed to run flat for far too long. We exact impossible demands from it: we want its tread to be as resilient as a Sherman Tank's, as delicate as a filo pastry shell. And when it runs too true, too smoothly, we actually get suspicious. Women fret over it, climbing out every few miles to inspect it. Men store it in their trunk, where it lies unused and barely acknowledged until you try to take it away from them. Then they're coming at you with a 4-way tire-iron, look out!

Why is our Love tire so precious?

Well, just think back to your childhood; to those care-free days when instead of riding around on *4 Tires of Living*, you were riding around on *3 Tires of Living*.

It's pretty obvious that when you're a kid the Candy Tire is *the* pivotal tire of your day-to-day existence, far out-weighing in importance its two lesser counterparts. Candy (sugar) is the supreme manifestation of Love. When you're a kid and someone—anyone—gives you candy, that's it, brother, you *love* them. And, you figure, *they* love *you*, because *why else would they be giving you candy?* Thus, the childhood pursuit of candy *is* the pursuit of Love.

This correlation never completely disappears. As adults when we fall in love with someone we sort of think of them as a Big Sugary Snack and give them names like "sweetie," "sugarpie" and "honeybun."

That's why our Love Tire is our most sentimental tire. We've been riding on it ever since we can remember. Career, Mental and Physical Health, Spirituality, those tires come later. Love is the Big Wheel.

O.K. So You Got Dumped

It's quite possible you've almost become comfortable being heartbroken. Maybe you're a little frightened to change. But remember *change* is always inevitable. Even as you are sitting here reading this, you are changing. The atoms in your body are constantly in motion, creating energy.

All life, with the possible exception of Ed McMahon, is just energy pretending to be doing something.

Nature hates a vacuum. Get off your butt.

Tip for the Day

For many people, their worst fear is being alone. But being alone doesn't necessarily mean being lonely. Remember, loneliness is the emptiness of being alone. But solitude is the fulfillment of being alone. If you want to enjoy loneliness and solitude at the same time, try masturbating!

Torching

Six weeks is sufficient time for agonizing over a broken heart. After that, it's over. Forget it and move on. The worst thing you can do is sit around and obsess about what went wrong. What went wrong is It Didn't Work Out. Done deal. You were vulnerable enough to allow someone to see the real you, and they fled screaming in the opposite direction. Well, that's *their* problem.

In the end, you know what it boils down to? The person wasn't your soul-mate. See, nature always produces her miracles in pairs. We all have a complement, a dreamboat, a person whose heart, when we meet them, will meld with ours and beat as one forever.

Unfortunately, the "soul-mate" ideal is one of God's crueler jokes because, though matches are made in heaven, *we're* down here on earth, and there's five billion of us. For all you know, your soul-mate is hunched over a dung fire in Bhutan right now cooking goat meat. In other words, if you can't even find a decent roommate for your aunt, how can you possibly expect to find your soul-mate?

Tip for the Day

When someone says, "It's better to have loved and lost than never to have loved at all," keep in mind you're talking to a loser. Try to find someone who's never loved at all and get their side of the story.

Scientific Reasoning
(For Why You Got Dumped)

Like I said, it's wrong to obsess about your breakup, but I don't think sitting down and trying to come up with some charts, graphs and mathematical calculations for why you got dumped could hurt.

The *only* reason I'm exploring this is because I just came across an enlightening scientific study that pointed out when women fall in love, they fall in love "ears-first." In other words, they fall in love with a man's whispers, promises and endearments.

I have to believe this because it was in *Cosmopolitan*.

I can tell you that when I fell in love, it was with every one of my senses *except* hearing. I did a lot of ogling, sniffing, pawing and licking, but I never *heard* a single word she had to say.

The Love Pie below depicts the geometric configuration of our romance.

See? Combining our incomplete sensory components created a Total Sensory Experience. Sort of like the log flume ride at Six Flags. Of course, it was easy to mistake this for love.

PARTS OF ME THAT RESPONDED   PARTS OF HER THAT RESPONDED

These are the reasons my girlfriend gave for leaving me:

"Liar"

"Incommunicative"

"Make noises in my sleep like I swallowed some aquarium gravel."

Notice how they're all hearing-related? She never gave her other senses a chance to get to know me!

Tip for the Day

Everyone, at the beginning of a romance, lies. You have to. It's a way of covering your insecurities and presenting yourself in the best light possible.

But every lie is a "debt" you eventually have to pay back. This is why it's a good idea to keep track of all your lies in a notebook. Because the only thing worse than lying is forgetting you lied and being called on it.

Eventually, you will have to consolidate all your lies under one big Umbrella Lie. Try this one:

> *"When we first met, I was taking an experimental hay fever drug called Alledrone, and one of the side effects is an overactive imagination. So, I might have told you I once drummed for Pearl Jam, but that's because I really believed I drummed for Pearl Jam. The stuff just makes me lie. It's not my fault. It's Parke Davis'."*

So You've Got a Broken Heart

99% of the time, the reason Love didn't work was because it wasn't Love in the first place. It was In-Love (A Total Sensory Experience).

Before you go off and fall in love again, do yourself a favor. Go down to the local hardware store and buy a wooden 6-foot paint ladder. When you get the ladder home, take a black marker and write on the bottom step, in big letters, the word "ALONE". On the next step, write the word "INTERACTION." On the next, write "ATTRACTION." On the next, write "ROMANCE." When you get to that big, fold-out platform where the paint cans are supposed to sit—the thing that says "This is not a step!"—write "IN-LOVE." Then, at the top of the ladder write "LOVE."

Now start slowly climbing the ladder. Notice how each rung gets a little more exciting and precarious! When you step on the IN-LOVE platform, pause and take in the panoramic splendor. Oops...

You idiot! You knew all along "IN-LOVE" was not a step! But you thought it would support you, didn't you? And, before you knew it, you came crashing down, dribbling your chin on every rung until you hit ALONE again—not knowing what it's like to reach LOVE.

From now on, before you go looking for LOVE, take the Ladder Test. It's an eloquent reminder that IN-LOVE is *not* a step.

Tip for the Day

Remember, love is not heart-shaped. It's circular.
That's why it's so difficult to distinguish between a well-rounded person and a BIG FAT ZERO.

Love Dynamics

My Aunt Gretel likes to say, "Love makes the world go around," but, of course, she's never explained how.

I'll bet if you asked my ex-girlfriend, her explanation would be something like:

"The male wheel pulls the female wheel along by means of a chain of endearments, promises, macho posturings and self-important diatribes linked by long periods of total silence."

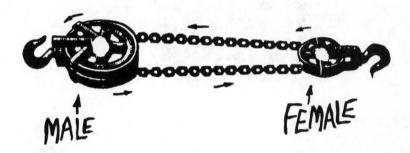

PULLEY SYSTEM

But, if you asked my ex-girlfriend's therapist, she would probably say something like:

"Love should be an efficient operation in which two well-rounded, independent wheels operate tandemly, enjoying the dynamics of their synchronous meshing."

Boy, are therapists ever full of it! I'll stick with my charts and graphs.

MALE   FEMALE

GEAR SYSTEM

Tip for the Day

When your relationship reaches a super crumbly stage, your girlfriend may try to convince you the two of you need to see a therapist. You have every right to be horrified, but you owe it to her to try.

It's like when you're driving around in circles hopelessly lost and she's pleading with you to pull into a gas station to ask for directions. You can't make her understand the "male problem-solving thing." Eventually, you do pull into the gas station.

Well, that's all therapy is—stopping to ask for a little direction. It's really not all that bad as long as you wait in the car while she goes inside to do all the asking.

How Long Should Love Last?

There is a universal explanation for why relationships fail, but it differs according to who's doing the explaining:

Female Point of View: "He turned into an asshole."

Male Point of View: "I don't know, she just kinda went nuts on me."

For this reason alone, it's ridiculous to expect to love someone the rest of your life. The biggest mistake you can make is to buy the storybook notion that love lasts forever. Love lasts until you turn into an asshole or go nuts.

Tip for the Day

Before you get involved in a romantic relationship, go out and buy a medium-sized bottle of tabasco sauce. Every time you're staring at your burger or taco, reflecting on the great sex (and intimacy!) you just had, sprinkle a few drops on your meal. After the first few months, you'll find yourself thinking, "Boy oh boy, we sure are going through a lot of tabasco sauce..." Then you'll notice the depletion level subsiding. Eventually the bottle is about two-thirds empty. Sure, you keep putting it out there on the table, but sort of as a courtesy, and neither of you reach for it except maybe to read the label and mutter something like, "Hmmm tabasco company, New Iberia, Louisiana. I wonder if that's any-where near New Orleans..."

How Long Should Love Last If You Don't Like Tabasco Sauce?

We can learn a lot about love from songwriters. They are experts on heartbreak, and, in fact, have heartbreak "quotas."

Take a look at any current popular singer/songwriter. John Mellencamp, Don Henley, Roseanne Cash, Bonnie Raitt, to name a few. On any given album there's an average of four songs that are about getting your heart stomped on.

If the recording artist releases one album per year, that's 4 stomped hearts from 4 different love affairs—roughly one stomp every 3 months. These songwriters are professionals. They're paid to be in touch with their emotions, so it's pretty safe to say a good healthy life span for a relationship is 3 months.* Anything after that is gravy.

Tip for the Day

A good heartbreak needs about three solid days of total subterranean despair. Pick a nice floor, lie down on it and listen to the Smiths nonstop for 72 hours. Just stare up at the ceiling and let Morrissey's bleatings swaddle you in despondency. Pretty soon you'll be thinking, "Compared to this guy, I got no problems."

---

*Figure 2 months if you live in a rural area, since country/western albums average 6 stomped-heart songs per album.

P.S.I.'s: Positive Self Images

There's nothing like rejection to make you feel as worthless as a Louisiana hazardous material dump. What you need right now is to get some self-esteem into your tires.

Somewhere at the bleak juncture where my girlfriend dumped me, my House of Index Cards, Inc. turned into a debacle and I was thinking about shrinkwrapping myself to death, I decided to crack open a stack of cards (Pink 8-1/2 pt. Broadway-lined) and tried listing the things I still liked about myself. A few of them were:

> I'm too young to die. I'm a man-teen!
>
> I make a fried Spam and horseradish sandwich that once got a mention in *Redbook Magazine's* Recipe-rama.
>
> I am assertive. Like when I have to explain to my 82-year-old Aunt Gretel that she needs to move out of my apartment and be her own woman.
>
> I am not ashamed to admit I read *Redbook*.
>
> I have three more months left on my storage unit and enough index cards to write a book.

Well, sir, it didn't take long before I had a whole cardstack of things I liked about myself! I call those cards my P.S.I.'s: Positive Self Images—and I encourage you to start making some of your own. *

---

* If you find that you've run short of index cards, I'm a pretty reliable source— at reasonable bulk prices!

As a warmup, below, write down 32 things you like about yourself, but write them in pencil so you can erase them later. I know how self-help books often end up in used book stores and yard sales, and nobody wants to pay 50 cents to find somebody else's weird, disembodied scribblings all over the pages. I have, however, filled in a few "universalities" to help you get started.

Things I Like About Myself

1 *opposable thumbs*   17 _____
2 _____   18 _____
3 _____   19 *already 14 pages into a*
4 _____   *self-help book!!*
5 _____   20 _____
6 _____   21 _____
7 _____   22 _____
8 _____   23 _____
9 _____   24 _____
10 _____   25 _____
11 _____   26 _____
12 _____   27 _____
13 _____   28 _____
14 _____   29 _____
15 _____   30 _____
16 _____   31 _____
                           32 _____

Reactionary Behavior

Now that you're on the road to positive self-esteem, don't get caught up in reactionary behavior. For example, be careful about badmouthing your ex—telling all your friends what a Big Fat Zero he was—which is what my girlfriend did. Pretty soon, she actually started to believe her own INCREDIBLY DISTORTED FABRICATIONS and forgot it was just a defense. And once she began to believe these BULBOUSLY INFLATED WHOPPERS, she went out and got involved with someone exactly 180 degrees opposite of me, someone who has the personality of a blanched almond—my dry cleaner for chrissakes—probably because he's a predictable in-by-8-out-by-5 drone, who emits toluene.

However, I will stop short of badmouthing my dry cleaner because I know what we dislike in others is what we dislike in ourselves. When my ex-girlfriend calls me a Big Fat Zero, it means she truly loathes *herself*. It's obvious she still cares about me.

I'll bet I know what those two talk about when they're together—my clothes.

Tip for the Day

Here's something that inflates your self-esteem every time.

Take out an ad in the Personals column of your newspaper to announce to the world what a winner you are.

"Hey, everyone, I'm a (status, gender), intelligent, unique, sophisticated and my own person. I know the passion in exotic travel and the intimacy of a quiet evening at home. I don't judge, and I don't play games. I am affectionate, witty, nurturing and guess what? NO ONE'S GETTING A PIECE OF ME! UNDERSTAND? I'VE GOT IT WAY TOO TOGETHER. I DON'T NEED NOBODY. STARE ALL YOU WANT FOLKS, IT AIN'T FOR SALE!"

The newspaper won't even know what to do. They'll have to put you under your own heading: "People Not Seeking Anyone."

Big Fat Zeros

There are basically two types of Big Fat Zero Boyfriends: Ones who ignore their girlfriends and ones who expect their girlfriends to be their moms.

The woman who constantly gets involved with the first type is repeating a pattern she grew up with. She is attracted to guys who, like her dad, habitually ignored her. She believes if she can change the Big Fat Zero Boyfriend, she can rectify her childhood.

The other kind of Big Fat Zero expects his girlfriend to make up for his mom's lack of caretaking. But, in actuality, Mom was too busy covering for Dad's (Big Fat Zero, Sr.) absenteeism.

Understand what I'm saying? Men who want women to be their moms *really* want those women to be their dads.

Thus, the best kind of woman for this type of Big Fat Zero is a woman who wants *him* to be *her* dad. That way, the Big Fat Zero would be a dad to the woman who's his dad. In other words the guy would be his *own* grandfather (Old Jedidiah Zero).

Tip for the Day

Sooner or later your partner may try to pin you to the wall with one of those questions like:

"Would you still love me if I got run over by a bus and became a vegetable?"

Nip that one right in the bud and say, "Hell, no! Of course not." Because if you say "yes," well, they're going to get just a little too careless, a little too cocky, and next thing you know, they'll be out there flitting around in the street, playing chicken, yelling, "C'mon and try to hit me, Mr. Bus Driver! I got Love Insurance!"

Male Sensitivity

Scenario: You have a date with Sheila. When Sheila was 8, her father, a classic rageaholic, threw her out of the house for leaving her Big Wheel tricycle in the front yard. Abandoned and alone, she spent the night in a henhouse, surrounded by feral, clucking chickens. This left an emotional scar.

You show up for the date with Sheila in a rented limo. She greets you at the door, you hand her some flowers and remark that she looks lovely. At that very moment, a 350-lb biker named Tiny roars into the front yard on a chopper and announces he's taking her to the Omelette Hut. Sheila blows past you and breezes off with Tiny. Who's the insensitive dirtbag?

You are! Tiny was intuitive enough to realize Sheila needed "closure" for her traumatic childhood incident. His thoughtful and reassuring actions said to her, "It's *o.k.* to park a bike in the yard." Accompanying her to the Omelette Hut (metaphorically a henhouse) filled the void of abandonment created by her father. You're just a guy standing there with some flowers and an overpriced rental car—superficial gestures.

Tip for the Day

As soon as we start to like someone, two little gremlins appear on our shoulders. The one on the right says, "Take advantage of their insecurities and frailties, and you will win their love." The gremlin on the left says, "Try to accept their insecurities and frailties, and you will win their love." If we listen to the "take advantage" gremlin, we turn into assholes. But if we listen to the "try to accept" gremlin and it turns out we can't handle the enormity of their insecurities and frailties, well, we're perceived as "going nuts on them."

Furthermore, when we break up with someone, we never really tell them the truth about why we're breaking up, because that would be too devastating or an admission we took advantage of them. Either way, it stinks.

So, if someone breaks up with you, don't spend a lot of time lying around trying to figure out why. You don't really want to know. Somebody listened to the wrong gremlin, that's all.

Getting Over It

I remember the day I finally got over my heartbreak.

I was standing in line to buy some Lotto tickets. There was a fellow in front of me. I watched, curiously, as he purchased a dozen Pick-6 Scratch-off tickets, *partially* uncovered each one, then threw it in the trash can.

"Pardon me," I said to him. "I couldn't help notice you're not playing the whole ticket. How do you expect to win the 61-million-dollar jackpot?"

"I don't care about winning the jackpot," he replied. "I just love watching the numbers unfold. And if those first two or three numbers match, I quit right there. Then I get to walk around imagining I really did have a jackpot winner, which is an exciting thought to carry with you all day."

He nudged my shoulder. "The possibility," he said, winking, "is always more rewarding than the pay-off." Watching him walk away, I realized something: people are like lottery tickets. To watch someone unfold before us—spiritually, emotionally and intellectually—well, that's what a "relationship" really is, and it doesn't matter if that person turns out not to be your soul-mate or "jackpot" because that wasn't the point in the first place. We accept them for what they are—a beautiful unfolding human.

I knew then I was ready to go looking for love again. Just as soon as I was done fishing through that trash can.

Tip for the Day

We let the word "love" seduce us. We hear it so much in our lives, myth and music that its power far exceeds its potential.

For most of us, hearing the word "love" is more important than what's behind it. Sure, we want the "caring" and "feeling" stuff, but if it doesn't come wrapped in that shiny, satin gift wrap paper called "love" we won't accept it.

You know what a mightier word than "love" would be? "Loke," which is "love" and "like" combined. But, if someone gazed into your eyes and said, "Baby, I loke you," you'd just walk away laughing like a hyena. Tragically, you would have frittered away a gift greater than love itself. God, are we spoiled.

Forgiveness

If *I* can muster up the courage to forgive my ex-girl-friend, you can forgive your ex too.

Forgiving someone is one of the hardest things you'll ever have to do because it means you can no longer walk around hanging that person from a mental meathook and taking shots at them with a whiffle ball bat. It means you have to clean the slate and go out and make new blunders with new people.

Or maybe get it right for a change.

The best way to forgive your ex is to do it over the phone. Just blurt, "I forgive you," and hang up quickly. You can even leave it on the answering machine.

When I called up my old girlfriend to forgive her, I actually got a wrong number—the Xi Thuc Zhan residence. But I followed through and forgave Mr. Thuc Zhan. He sounded relieved.

Try calling up strangers from the phone book and forgiving them. Not only will it loosen you up for the crucial real thing, the strangers will feel better. Everyone likes to know they're forgiven.

Tip for the Day

Let's defuse one myth right now. Nobody "falls" in love. Nope, we see it right there in front of us. Though it's just a puddle, we back up, take a running start and execute a triple-and-a-half gainer headfirst right into it.

Admit it. You didn't fall. You dove and got hurt. Otherwise you'd be suing the hell out of somebody.

First Impressions

Ever notice the things that initially attract you to someone eventually become their most horrible traits? A woman may be attracted to a man because he's "independent." But, six months later his "independence" comes off as distance and lack of feeling, like Clint Eastwood on Nyquil.

At first, they make love like there's no tomorrow. He makes her feel *so* sexy and desirable. Six months later, they're reading tabasco labels.

Conversely, a guy may be attracted to a woman for her "emotional intensity." Three months later, he realizes it's not "intensity," it's "instability"!

Get it? *It's a big mistake to trust your initial attraction.*

Since all the things that you first like about someone go rancid, doesn't it stand to reason that things you hate about someone will start to grow on you?

When I started dating again, I made it a point to be thoughtful, caring, a good listener and above all, to make women feel admired and respected. Naturally these niceties allowed the relationships to blossom and in no time, boy was I making them miserable!

A few weeks ago, I had a blind date. To hell with it! I said and showed up dressed as a Visigoth. Alternately referring to my date as "wench" and "Sabine Woman," I jumped up and down on her couch until the frame broke, locked her in a closet and rifled through her drawers. We made plans to see each other again. On the next date, she answered the door dressed in a sarong and irrigation boots. She referred to me all evening long as "a worthless chunk of frozen blue air waste." I think it's going to work!

Tip for the Day

I suppose for most women the ideal man, "Mr. Right," would be handsome, sexy, affectionate, self-assured, witty and extremely attentive to her needs. Well, good luck trying to find him, sister.

Maybe you need to adjust your criteria. Try replacing "handsome" and "sexy" with "bald" and "wearing a t-shirt." Now, instead of looking for Mr. Right, you're looking for Mr. Clean which shouldn't be too much of a problem.

All Women Love Attention

You can never give a woman too many gifts! A gift always says, "I was thinking about you, and I care a lot." But the most memorable gifts are those that say, "I was thinking about you, and I'd really feel awful if you died." In other words, it's a gift that makes her life safer. Here are some sure-fire winners:

A brand new set of steel belted all-weather radials

A radon detector

Pepper mace for fending off grizzlies

Orange reflective clothing of any kind

But always include flowers or poetry! You don't want to give the impression you're unsentimental.

Tip for the Day

If you find it difficult or impossible to write poetry, do what I do. Get out that old trigonometry book from high school, find some choice theorems and arrange them in poetic form. Hint: Every time you see the word "angle," change it to "angel."

Example:

I complement you, angel,
and define you infinitely. I am your
adjacent angel. You are my
cosine.
I denote you factorially.
I am the
curve generated by the motion of your
point.

Oh! Acute angel.

How to Get Someone to Fall in Love with You!

Wouldn't it be great if we possessed some kind of Love Velcro, something that could get whomever we wanted to stick to us?

Well, some of us do. And it's powerful stuff!

But rather than tell you about it, why don't I show you? Why don't I set you up on a date with someone who possesses this amazing Love Velcro? I promise you by the date's end you'll already be feeling the first tugs and pangs of love. Ready?

We'll call your date A.G. All you need to know about A.G. is that A.G. *loves* conversation. It won't be an exciting date, no fancy restaurants or sexy night spots. But, boy, will you two talk. So, have a great time! (And I'll want a full report on you two kids in the morning!)

Your Date with A.G.

"Hi there, I'm A.G. I've heard a lot about you. How was your day today?"

"_____."

"Really? Look, I'm not too good at small talk so why don't you just go ahead and tell me about all the people who wrecked your childhood?"

"_____

_____."

"No kidding? That's awful. Tell me more."

"_____."

"I think I know how you feel. My, that's a lot of hurt for one person. But it's over and done with. You know what? I see a lot of *passion* inside you, just screaming to get out. Tell me about your hopes and desires."

"_____

_____."

"No! I don't think that's weird at all. Besides who am I to judge?

"Hot diggetty, look at the time! I'd really love to do this again. Why, we hardly talked about me at all..."

End of Date

Don't tell me. You've never met anyone so under-standing, so willing to let you unburden your soul without fear of judgment. Well, Love Velcro just means listening. If you honestly took the time to share your intimate feelings with A.G., you can't help but feel yourself falling in love.

Remember, love has very little to do with compatibility, charm, chemistry, respect, personality or honesty. That's just window dressing! Love comes, quite simply, when we listen.

Oh, by the way, say hello to A.G. ➡

I really had a great time! XXX Gretel

* Aunt Gretel is currently available for a romantic encounter and possible live-in situation. You may contact her through the publisher.

Tip for the Day

I forgot to tell you. Intense discussion doesn't create two-way intimacy. Saying, "We need to talk about our relationship. I think there's a problem," might draw you closer to your boyfriend, but it makes him nervous. "Why is she talking about the relationship?" he thinks. "She should be talking about me!"

But if you said, "We need to talk about the refrigerator. I think there's a problem," he would perk right up.

Remember:

Women achieve intimacy through intense conversation.

Men achieve intimacy through making sandwiches.

Ask a guy to recall an intimate moment (other than sex), and he'll probably answer something like, "When my girlfriend and I made Spam and horseradish sandwiches."

Men cannot experience intimacy unless snacks are involved. Thus, if you want him to address the relationship, it has to be while you're making sandwiches.

Write down what you want from the relationship on 3 x 5 cards: "Affection," "Honesty," "Communication," whatever... Take the 3 x 5 cards and plaster them over the labels of all your condiments, like mayonnaise or pickle relish.

It's only a matter of time before he'll be asking concernedly, "Hey, where's all the affection?" or "We need more commitment."

What Women Really Want

What women really want is to be understood. Men are constantly trying to be encyclopedias or repairmen or chart graphers. Women want them to feel.

This is the great tragic line that will always separate the sexes: men explaining the superficial nature of things to women who would much rather see the emotion beneath it.

You're wrong if you think women don't want to hear what "torque" is or how the NBA draft works. But when they ask, "How does the NBA draft work?" you've got to be prepared to explain the passion behind the NBA draft. And if by the end of the explanation there's not a lump in your throat and fire in your belly—if you haven't made them understand that the NBA draft can break a man's heart or make him happy beyond all dreams—well, my friend, you've simply wasted your breath.

Tip for the Day

It's important for men to be understood, too. I'm not talking about feelings or emotions or stuff. I just mean they need to be understood. For example, if a man goes down on one knee and says, "Will you marry me?", don't stare at him blankly and ask, "Who's William Aramy?" Try to understand him for crying out loud.

How to Satisfy a Woman Every Time

Lick, paw, ogle, caress, praise, pamper, relish, savor, massage, empathize, serenade, compliment, support, dig, floralize, feed, laminate, tantalize, bathe, humor, placate, stimulate, jiffylube, stroke, console, bark, purr, hug, baste, marinate, coddle, excite, pacify, tattoo, protect, phone, correspond, anticipate, nuzzle, smooch, toast, minister to, forgive, sacrifice, ply, accessorize, leave, return, beseech, sublimate, entertain, charm, lug, drag, crawl, tunnel, show equality for, spackle, oblige, fascinate, attend, implore, bawl, shower, shave, ululate, trust, dip, twirl, dive, grovel, ignore, defend, milk, coax, clothe, straddle, melt, brag, acquiesce, aromate, prevail, super collide, fuse, fizz, rationalize, detoxify, sanctify, help, acknowledge, polish, upgrade, spoil, reddi-whip, embrace, delouse, accept, butter-up, hear, understand, jitterbug, mosh, locomote, beg, plead, borrow, steal, climb, swim, hold her hair while she's puking in the toilet, nurse, resuscitate, repair, patch, crazyglue, respect, entertain, calm, allay, kill for, die for, do a nickel in Attica for, dream of, promise, exceed, deliver, tease, flirt, enlist, torch, pine, wheedle, cajole, angelicize, murmur, snuggle, snoozle, snurfle, hezbollah, jihad, elevate, enervate, alleviate, spotweld, serve, rub, rib, salve, bite, taste, nibble, gratify, take her to Funkytown, scuttle like a crab on the ocean floor of her existence, diddle, doodle, hokey-pokey, hanky-panky, crystal blue persuade, flip, flop, fly, don't care if I die, swing, slip, slide, slather, mollycoddle, squeeze, moisturize, humidify, lather, tingle, slamdunk, keep on rockin' in the free world, wet, slicken, undulate, gelatinize, brush, tingle, dribble, drip, dry, knead, fluff, fold, blue-coral wax, ingratiate, indulge, wow, dazzle, amaze, flabbergast, enchant, idolize and worship, and then go back, Jack, and do it again.

How to Satisfy a Man Every Time:

Show up.

Stinky Dead Love

I believe good memories have a longer shelf life than bad memories, which is why a year or so after splitting up, couples forget *why* they split up and get these wistful notions of getting back together. To understand why this is a mistake is to understand a little about fishing.

When you reflect on a great fishing trip, you remember lolling about beside a gorgeous river or lake, basking in sunshine, serenity and the warm company of buddies. You also remember the fish you landed. And what a trophy it was! That fish lived gloriously and passionately for about three more minutes, then it died. Shortly thereafter it started to decompose.

The difference between love and loving is the same as between fish and fishing. If you get back together with your old flame, you might do some fishing. But, in the end, you'll be driving home alone with the day's memories behind you and one big dead stinky fish in the back seat.

Tip for the Day

How come there isn't a Lonely Street in every town? And, at the end of it, a Heartbreak Hotel? A place where broken men could go and be so lonely they could die?

Actually, forget Lonely Street. Cul-de-sacs are notoriously poor business locations. Better to put it at the Interstate off-ramp, where everyone can find it, broken-hearted truckers and all. And call it the Heartbreak Residence Suites! With little kitchen set-ups, free breakfast, and maid service because we're gonna be there a long time.

Boy, Elvis really missed the boat on this idea!

Respect

How often are you driving along, and come across a huge piece of tire tread lying in the road? You know what that is? Lost respect.

Respect is a very durable material. Every one of our tires is built on it. Respect sustains our Love Tire and our Career Tire. Self-respect is the foundation of mental stability. Respect for nature or a higher force makes us Spiritual.

See, it doesn't matter if your tire is flat, misaligned or hanging on by one wobbly locknut. If the tread is still there, it's salvageable. Don't give up!

And if your partner is walking out on you, by all means, stop her and say, "Wait, we've still got tread."

But if she leaves, that's it. Don't grovel, for that would be leaving your *own* self-respect, your tread, in the middle of the road.

Tip for the Day

Look, I don't encourage the heckling of entertainers, but if you're in Vegas watching Dean Martin and all of a sudden he starts singing "You're Nobody ('Til Somebody Loves You)," I don't think it's wrong to stand up and shout, "Wait a minute, Mr. Martin. Are you saying everything I've done with my life is a waste…just because love hasn't come along? Well, I think not, Deano. Maybe I'm not a big-time show biz guy like you. Maybe I never played Matt Helm, but I am somebody, with or without love. And I will not allow you to undermine my self-worth!"

That's not heckling. That's standing up for your self-respect.

Never Give Up on Love!

Remember how I said our lives rest on four tires? Well, of the four tires, the one that will get the most wear and tear is the Love Tire. It will go through the rockiest terrain. It will have to grip the road better, ride steadier and last longer than all your other tires combined.

But if it blows, my friend, then it blows. You just ride it out. And when it's over, you get out, open the trunk, pop on that spare tire full of self-esteem and get back on the road.

Yes, love is a tire. And, even if it's bald and treadless, it's *your* Love Tire. I know that's not romantic, but if you *really* want to see something sad, take a walk down to the water and look at all those old tires nailed to the side of the dock. They're the pathetic, unrealistic tires waiting for their dreamboat to come in.

Tip for the Day

If you're lonely and want to talk to someone, instead of paying three dollars a minute to call a 900 number, try a 901 number. There are probably lots of people in Western Tennessee who wouldn't mind talking to you.

YOUR MENTAL-PHYSICAL TIRE

"There are just two things in life.
But I forget what they are."

\- John Hiatt

Your Mental-Physical Tire

Your Mental-Physical Tire is the driver's side, rear tire. Most people pay slightly more attention to this tire than the others because it's so easy to take care of. Mental and Physical are concepts we understand, even if we do constantly set them spinning in the ethereal mud and end up coated with the bleak slag of our everyday setbacks and depressions. *

Determining If You Suffer from Depression

It's sometimes difficult to tell if you're suffering from depression because it's a physical condition as well as a mental one. Quite often, people think their problem is depression when actually the problem has to do with *decompression* (the feeling of being underwater with 4000 pounds per square inch of water pressure against your eardrums.)

As you can see from the chart below, the characteristics of depression and decompression are almost identical.

Signs of Depression
1. Fear
2. Isolation
3. Lack of Concentration
4. Fatigue and General Malaise
5. Low Self-Esteem

Signs of Decompression:
1. Fear
2. Isolation
3. Lack of Concentration
4. Fatigue and General Malaise
5. Bubbles

---

* I don't know exactly what that means, but it sounds as if it should be in a self-help book.

So there. Maybe it's not the blues you have but the "bends." Before wasting thousands of dollars on psychiatric help, try holding your nose and blowing air out of your ears. If after this, you feel better, congratulations! You were never depressed to begin with!

Tip for the Day

The reason so many of us get depressed around Christmas time is from seeing all those Santa decorations. It reminds us of that horrible moment when we discovered He didn't really exist. He was our very most beloved and trusted childhood figure, but, hey, He's dead now and all those lights and plastic reindeer, well that's just rubbing it in.

Life Scripts

People who experience moments of crazed euphoria followed by long episodes of abject misery are manic-depressive. Most of us, however, are what I call Mannix-Depressive.

We all know people who repeatedly get themselves into predicaments *we* can see coming a mile away. It's almost as if they are following a script. Usually the script is like a "Mannix" episode. Every week Mannix ended up getting his butt kicked at some abandoned dockside, and he never quite understood why. *We* could see the script unfolding but *he* couldn't because he was trapped inside it. We would yell, "Look out Mannix! You're gonna get your butt kicked again!" Of course, he never heard us.

Mannix-Depressives know what they're doing but can't seem to do much about it. And it's making them miserable!

If you're trapped in a self-repeating script, it's time for rewrites. It's time to poke your head out of the dressing room and scream, "Who wrote this shit?"

Tip for the Day

How to Find a Therapist: Obviously, the best recommendation is from someone who was really screwed up but appears to be getting better. Otherwise, try the phone book. Avoid the ones at the top of the list like Aaron the Therapist, Attaboy Therapy or All Points Therapy. They're just trying to get the lazy customers.

Addictions

"Mannix-Depressive" behavior quite often signifies an addiction. Until you acknowledge your addictions, you'll never escape your life script.

Why not take a moment to jot down on individual 3 x 5 cards all the things you have no control over.

Examples:
>My obsession with my ex-girlfriend
>>(the Dumper).
>My workaholism.
>My financial dependence on my
>>foul-mouthed Aunt Gretel.
>And so on.

Study the cards for a moment, then go back to each one and add the phrase:
AND IT'S KICKING MY BUTT!
Congratulations. You're rewriting!

Tip for the Day

Remember, there's a difference between habits and addictions. For example, if your wife has bought a brand new glass living-room table and you keep putting your feet on it, that's a habit. If you keep putting your nose on it, that's an addiction.

Find Your Higher Power

Even though Mannix got his butt kicked every week, he always managed to triumph by the end of the episode! It seemed there was a higher power that always watched over Mannix and saved him so we could look forward to seeing him again the following week.

Likewise, the things you have no control over are the things *you* have to turn over to a higher power.

Find your higher power.

If the concept of your higher power seems a little fuzzy, try putting a name and a face to it. My suggestion is Mike Connors.

Mike Connors was the actor who played Mannix. See, Mannix was always trapped in the script, but Mike Connors actually had some say in what happened to Mannix. Thus, Mike Connors was Mannix's higher power.

Why not let him be yours too? He probably wouldn't mind—he strikes me as a really nice guy.

Write to: Mike Connors (Mannix)
14200 Ventura Blvd., Suite 106
Sherman Oaks, CA 91423

Send him all your 3 x 5 "Kicking My Butt" cards and tell him, "These aren't my problems anymore, they're yours!" Also, be sure to ask for some autographed pictures saying "Your higher power, Mike Connors" (send a SASE).

Tip for the Day

Get up every morning with a purpose, not a reason. If you don't know the difference, picture a robbery taking place in an alley. The guy holding the gun is being "purposeful." The guy forking over his wallet is being "reasonable."

MY HIGHER POWER, MIKE CONNORS

Daily Affirmations

Now is a good time to begin a practice of Daily Affirmations. An affirmation is a statement that says something good about yourself. You might even think of it as a prayer to yourself.

There are many collections of Daily Affirmations available at your bookstore but they're kind of expensive. I prefer "Natural Affirmations," ones found in your general surroundings. The other day I found a beautiful Natural Affirmation on the bulletin board of my neighborhood laundromat. It read:

"I HAUL TRASH!"

Why, the robust fellow who wrote this even included his name, phone number and the best time to call.

"I Haul Trash!" I repeated to myself. "Now that's genius." It was a perfect Natural Affirmation because it seemed to mean many things. It implied the cleansing of personal turmoils. It suggested action, change, improvement. It even had an environmental resonance to it. I repeated it many times that day, often to passing strangers.

Beginning today, try saying, "I Haul Trash" to yourself. Or look around for other natural affirmations. Some good ones I've come across are:

"I AM CURIOUS (YELLOW)"
"I AM NOT GOING TO PAY A LOT FOR THIS MUFFLER"
"I. MAGNIN"
"I AM GETTING READY TO RUMBLE"

Tip for the Day

Never buy affirmation books. They're just a collection of sentences without nouns.

I Am

The best affirmations begin with the words, "I am..." Boy, those are a couple of mighty words!

I guess one of my all-time favorite songs is *"I Am...I Said"* by the great Neil Diamond. It seems to me Neil really had nothing much to say after "I am...I said..." so he threw in some stuff about trying to talk to a chair and the chair not listening which makes no sense, but it didn't seem to matter because it sure was a monster hit and we all walked around singing "I am...I said," and kind of just mumbled over the part about the chair.

It says a lot about the power of the words "I am..." that Neil Diamond made such a huge hit with that song. If you just utter the words "I am..." well, anything you utter after that is gravy.

On a final note, I shudder to think what would have happened if Neil Young had gotten hold of that song, instead of Neil Diamond. It might not have been as affirming, but it would have had a lot more kickass guitar work!

Tip for the Day

I have discovered one of the best ways of overcoming depression is by doing something altruistic for others. No matter how crummy you feel, when you make others feel better, you feel better about yourself. And in doing so, you'll probably realize there are people out there with problems—I MEAN BIG PROBLEMS—that make yours look puny in comparison.

Homeless agoraphobics, for instance.

Material Things

Stop comparing yourself to others! The surest road to low self-esteem is to look around and convince yourself others are blessed with more. Or doing more. Or getting more!

On the lecture circuit I often meet people from small "real America" kinds of towns.

"Oh, it's a wonderful little town," they'll say. "And so friendly. Why, you don't even have to lock your doors at night!"

I have to admit I feel a little envious. But then I think to myself, if these people enjoy leaving their doors unlocked, they'd probably *really* enjoy carting all their belongings out into the front yard and leaving them there overnight.

I realize I'm talking to a person who gets some kind of feeble small-town thrill out of courting burglary every night. That's when my envy just disappears.

Tip for the Day

At the Elvis Impersonator's Convention in Las Vegas I talked with second-place finalist Sid Bunratty, age 35.

I asked him if he had been intimidated by the sheer number of impersonators. Sid's answer turned out to be one of the most inspiring things anyone has ever said to me.

"I don't have to be the best Elvis," said the 300-lb., 5'1" red-headed Irishman. "I only have to be the best Sid Bunratty." And that he was.

Why "Bad" Things Happen to "Good" People

We all know people who seem to have a "black cloud" following them. Maybe they're accident-prone, or constantly getting laid off. Maybe they get mugged a lot, continuously make bad investments, or get trampled every time they try to pet a large-hooved animal.

It's easy to look at these people and say they're unlucky. But, if you could really see inside them, you'd more than likely find a good deal of hidden anger. This anger may be directed at themselves or someone else, but either way, they're subconsciously putting out the welcome mat for trouble. For example, *every time* I buy a brand new suit I end up spilling mustard on it. Once I would have attributed this to bad luck and clumsiness, but knowing what I do now about repressed anger, I realize it's because I hate my dry cleaner.

You might have heard the story about the fellow who was supposed to fly from New York City to St. Croix with his fiancé to get married. They boarded a flight at LaGuardia and the plane ran off the runway into the East River. Dazed, but uninjured, they boarded another plane which dropped them in Miami in the middle of Hurricane Andrew. Well, they finally arrived in St. Croix only to discover their hotel had been hit by the same hurricane and their room was occupied—by looters!

Though on the surface it would appear to be a "string of bad luck," there was probably a lot of resentment and trepidation on the groom's part about his impending marriage. Boarding an ill-fated plane into a hurricane was his subconscious way of expressing it.

Work on getting in touch with your inner anger, and if my dry cleaner is reading this, he can go to hell!

Tip for the Day

People who chronically break the speed limit are acting out their intolerance of authority, namely law enforcement officers. And that's good!

If you enjoy speeding, try getting a personalized license plate with the word "VOID" on it. That way, when you get a speeding ticket, the officer will have to write "VOID" on the ticket.

Barnacleizing

The crab and the barnacle are supposed to live a symbiotic existence. The barnacle cleans parasites off the crab's back. As the crab scoots around the ocean floor, the barnacle gets a free ride.

Of course, the barnacle is never really going anywhere on his own initiative. He just gets dragged along to new locations, picking those same damn parasites. So it's always at best a working holiday. If you ask me, the barnacle is getting the raw end of the deal.

What about you?

Are you barnacleizing? Just picking at your parasitic depression? When I was depressed about my failed House of Index Cards venture, I spent a long time blaming myself for being a lousy businessman. I dwelled on my mistakes, replaying every bungled move in my head. I was barnacleizing. It occurred to me that there must have been some repressed anger in me that wanted me to fail.

But *then* I thought to myself: If people can sabotage themselves with their inner anger, they can probably sabotage *other* people with their inner anger.

That's when I realized, *Someone out there was sabotaging me!* Someone with a lot of inner anger. Someone who *didn't want my House of Index Cards to succeed*.

And I'm pretty sure I know who it was...the people who make those Post-It Notes!

Naturally, I can't really prove this in a court of law, but I'm *sure* it's true. And, you know what? I'm *glad* they willed me to fail. Because it taught me a valuable lesson: Failure is *never* your fault. There are secret angry forces out there causing you to fail.

So stop blaming yourself. Blame someone else. Anyone. Stop being a barnacle and start being a crab! It's time to make a move, even if it's sideways.

Tip for the Day

Remember, you can't suppress anger. It will mutate into something weirder. You have to deal with it the moment it crops up, even if it's unattractive, even if people think you're a jerk.

Everyone worries about the Middle East or the Balkans. "They're hotheads," we think to ourselves. But at least they're letting off steam. If you ask me, it's those little pockets of complacency on the planet where you'll find the real powder kegs, like the Quakers and the Amish. Boy, I don't want to be too close when they finally snap!

Effective Arguing

There's nothing wrong with arguing. In fact, it's a healthy way to release anger. But for crying out loud, stick to the point!

Whenever I buy a bottle of Dr. Bronner's soap at the Nature Rack and bring it home, you know what happens? I end up standing in the shower with the bottle in my hand reading all those "One God... all one... absolute cleanliness o.k.! All one-body-mind-soul Marx murdered 66 million..." diatribes on the label. Pretty soon the hot water runs out. Three or four hours later I realize I never actually got around to putting any soap on my body. Dr. Bronner's cryptic sermonizing distracted me from his point: To get people clean!

Tip for the Day

When your girlfriend is screaming at you, it's often hard to tell if she's angry or afraid. Think of her voice as an automobile horn. Short, staccato bursts mean anger. A long, harrowing wail, complete with Doppler effect, means smashup ahead!

Fear

It's time we talked about Fear—which is very closely related to Anger.

Below I have constructed a little Fear Scenario for you. Please be honest and careful in filling it out. Remember, it's not a test. There are no "right" or "wrong" answers, just choices. Afterwards, turn to the next page and study the Professional Analysis to see how your choices reflect your truest, darkest fears.

You are walking with your lover through a forest. Describe the forest (dense, rocky, uphill, etc.) _____. Suddenly you come across a bear. Does your partner stick by your side or run away? _____ The bear, in a voice not unlike Christopher Walken's, says something to you. What does it say? _____. Do you approach the bear or give it a wide berth? _____.

Later, as darkness descends, you come across a body of water and a shoehorn, which you recognize as belonging to your dad. You turn and see Dad beckoning to you. He is holding something in an outstretched palm, a chinchbug maybe. But as you near him he turns into a tree trunk. In one word, how does this make you feel?_____.

End of Scenario.

Tip for the Day

A lot of people don't know it, but Christopher Walken is an excellent dancer.

An Apology

Sorry, I *had* the Professional Analysis to the Fear Scenario, but I misplaced it somewhere.

Now if you feel hurt, angry or confused about that, it helps nail down my point—all fear is based on abandonment, the giving of our trust and attachment to others and seeing them let us down.

This all comes from your family: the dad who put up a wall, the mom who was always covering for dad's behavior, the grandfather who kept rambling off about freeloaders ("gravy people," my grandfather called them.) And, of course, Aunt Gretel, who at this very moment is calling my answering machine, probably from the Harriet Tubman Women's Shelter, to shake me down for the money I borrowed from her.

I don't care whaat anyone thinks. *I'm not* glomming off of Aunt Gretel's Gravy Train. She's just upset that I made her move out. But how do you explain to someone they're a nightmare to live with? Aunt Gretel fears she's been abandoned. Hey, I'm trying to find her a roommate!

Tip for the Day

If you're angry with or embarrassed by your family, the next time you buy a wallet, don't bother removing those "phony" pictures of relatives in the photo compartment. Just pretend those people are your family. You might try giving them names and little personal histories. Show the pictures to friends and say something like, "Here's my Uncle Roy. He's my favorite uncle." If the person you're showing the picture to becomes suspicious and says, "Wait a minute, I've seen that picture before..." explain Uncle Roy is a professional "wallet model."

Open Letters

Sometimes our Mental-Physical Tire gets whacked out of alignment from all the knocks we take from other people. That's when it's wise to use the tried and true therapy technique of sitting down and writing an open letter to those you feel have wronged you (or, in reality, have wronged *themselves*.) Here goes:

Dear Dad:

Years ago I wrote a script for an episode of The Lone Ranger. The script never aired, but if it had, I would have acted in it as well:

> SCENE: *TYPICAL DUSTY TOWN STREET. THE LONE RANGER HAS JUST PERFORMED ANOTHER HEROIC DEED. AS HE IS ABOUT TO RIDE AWAY, THE CYNICAL OLD TOWN DRUNK (ME!) STUMBLES AFTER HIM.*

CYNICAL TOWN DRUNK

"Hey, Lone Ranger, where are you running to *now*? Why don't you stick around and accept our gratitude? Or would that mean you'd have to *feel*?"

> THE LONE RANGER STOPS UNEASILY. TOWNSFOLK START TO GATHER. THE DRUNK FORTIFIES HIMSELF WITH ANOTHER PULL OF WHISKY.

CYNICAL TOWN DRUNK

"Why is it always on *your* terms, L.R.? Why do you always get to be the hero and we're just the fearful, helpless persons who can't do anything for ourselves? Does that make you feel goooooood? Does it make you feel like a biiiiiig man?"

THE SHERIFF ARRIVES AND TRIES TO WRESTLE HIM TO THE GROUND. SEVERAL TOWNSFOLK ASSIST.

CYNICAL TOWN DRUNK
(muffled, face down in the dirt)
"Ask him why he wears a mask! Ask him what he's hiding from! *Affection*, maybe?"

HE'S CARRIED AWAY IN A KICKSTORM OF DUST.

CYNICAL TOWN DRUNK
(off-camera)
"Just like my dad!"

THE LONE RANGER RIDES OFF INTO THE SUNSET. BUT INSIDE HE KNOWS HE'S REALLY THE LONELY RANGER.

Tip for the Day

We must accept Dad's shortcomings and forgive him. Dad couldn't be everything we wanted him to be.

My Dad never played catch with me. "I'm not much of a ball player," he would say, glumly, whenever I approached him with my ball and mitt. So I was left to my own devices, to toss the ball in the air or bounce it off the roof, his flat denial stinging in my ears, "...not much of a ball player."

I don't know which was worse, hearing those words from my Dad or hearing them from the thousands of fans who would come out to the ball-park and watch in astonishment as he beaned almost every batter he faced.

Later, I came to appreciate Dad's honesty. He really wasn't much of a ball player.

Not the Author's Intent

I just learned that a good self-help author always tells you where he's taking you, gets you there, then tells you where you've been. I'm sorry if I've been less than a gracious guide. This whole book-writing thing isn't the snap I thought it would be. First of all, puking up this past family experience stuff is uncomfortable enough, but I've also got ongoing problems like my displaced Aunt Gretel who reportedly has been hurling little complimentary bottles of shampoo at passersby from a third-story window at the Tubman Shelter. I've also got credit hounds nipping at my heels, an ex-girlfriend who's spreading around a load of bunkum about what a Big Fat Zero I am, and wait 'til you see the Tip for the Day. I am about one step away from climbing a clock tower, and, on top of all this, I'm supposed to be dispensing clinical advice to readers who, at $9.95 a pop ($12.95 Canadian), expect a self-help author to MAYBE HAVE IT FIGURED OUT BEFORE HE STARTS WRITING THE BOOK!

I'm really sorry. This whole thing has turned into one big clusterfuck.

Depression, Worry, Anger, Fear, Risk, Competence. That's the itinerary. Right now, we're supposed to be in Fear, but we have to go back to Worry, momentarily, and clear something up.

Urgent Tip for the Day

For some reason, Mike Connors has slapped a restraining order and harassment suit against me. As of this moment, you should no longer consider him your higher power. In fact, don't even mention his name! Please!

Your temporary higher power, until I can straighten everything out, is someone named Larry the Whispering Indian.

Worry and Anxiety

Worry is good. In fact, a worried mind is a good mind. If you worry that you worry too much, try imagining who you would be if you stopped worrying. Alfred E. Newman, that's who. A toothy benign weaselton of indeterminate age or purpose. To worry is to function.

What you want to try and avoid is anxiety. There is a big difference between worry and anxiety. If you throw all your problems in a washing machine and let them soak and agitate and they come out shrunken, that's worry. But, if the machine starts humming loudly, dancing across the floor and flashing OVERLOAD, *that's* anxiety.

Tip for the Day

In the early stages of anxiety, it's a good idea to make a videotape of yourself sleeping. That way, when you get insomnia, at least you can watch yourself asleep on TV while you're lying in bed wide awake.

Fear and Firewalking

Fear consists of two parts:

1. What's going to happen to me?

2. What *will others think* when it happens to me? In other words, the worst part of fear is being exposed.

If firewalking is designed to help you conquer fear, I can imagine other activities that would be far more effective and wouldn't leave you with bandaged feet.

For my money, the person who has truly mastered fear is the person who's not afraid to toss their clothes and stroll naked down the street.

Did you ever have that dream where you're trapped on a freeway median naked at rush hour, and all your Mom's church friends are passing by staring in horror?

Well, that dream, or a variation of it, will continue to haunt you until you've summoned the courage to act it out in real life. So forget all that macho Firewalking Warrior-Spirit crap. Just get naked and go take a walk in the neighborhood. But wear a watch so people will know you're rational, and not some kind of a kook.

Tip for the Day

The one surefire thing that outwits fear of failure is risk. Try this simple experiment: Pick a hot, crowded weekend afternoon and visit your community swimming pool. Go straight to the high-dive and execute a good solid 30-foot belly-flop. On the way down tell yourself "This is what failure feels like. This is what it's like to flop big time." Try to land with a loud thwack and splatter as many folks as possible. Afterwards, mingle among the poolsiders. You'll hear a lot of things, but the word "failure" won't be one of them.

Clear Mental Image

You can achieve anything if you form a clear mental image.

Do you know the Art Peplo story? Art was one of the fattest men alive. At one point, his weight reached 620 pounds! No matter what Art did, he could not stop eating. Art was so butt-heavy he could not fit through his own front door.

One day, Larry the Whispering Indian came to Art's rescue. Larry asked Art what, besides losing weight, he really wanted.

"Speak up," said Art, "I can't hear you." Larry repeated the question, "What do you really want?"

"I wanna go outside," he said. "I wanna see the blue sky and smell the fresh cut grass."

"Then picture yourself outside," whispered Larry.

And so Art pictured himself outside. In other words, he projected beyond losing weight. He kept a clear mental image of himself standing in his front yard, smelling the grass.

Six months later, a crowd of onlookers greeted Art Peplo as he took his first steps outside. Even though he had actually gained seven more pounds, it had finally occurred to him to widen his doorway; an idea that would probably not have happened had he not kept a clear mental image!

Tip for the Day

Dieting doesn't work.

If you can't change your self-image, try changing your image of food. Tell yourself all human suffering comes directly from food because Adam and Eve bit into the forbidden apple. Therefore, all food is evil. Before you bite into that fudge brownie, tell yourself, "Lucifer is in this brownie. I will not eat what Lucifer has baked!" That might work.

Saying No

Are you the kind of person who has trouble saying "no"? Do you feel you will lower someone's expectations if you say "no"? Do you fear hurting someone's feelings if you say "no"? Do you feel guilty if you say "no"?

Then try replacing "no" with the phrase, "Why don't you make me?"

Example 1: "Ed, how about going over these accounts?"

"Why don't you make me?"

Example 2: "Aunt Gretel, I would be delighted if you would join me for dinner this evening."

"Why don't you make me?"

Notice how this simple reply effectively shifts responsibility back to the person doing the asking? Try it!

On some occasions, "You and what army" works almost as well.

Tip for the Day

All life is negotiation. You barter, compromise, give and take, move the numbers around, trying to come away with a better deal. Yet, did it ever occur to you to stop and ask, "Can I just have it for free?"

Remember, that new car salesman or real estate agent probably doesn't want to be there any more than you do. The worst thing that he can say is "no." But, there's always a chance you're dealing with someone on the brink of snapping, someone thinking to themselves, "If this clown would just ask for the damn thing, I'd probably give it to him!"

"Can I just have it for free?" Seven words that take two-and-a-half seconds to utter. You can't afford not to ask.

Competence

At this point in the book, hopefully you've got your Mental and Physical Health Tire fairly well balanced and running smoothly. Enjoy the ride my friend! You are on the road to Competence. You drove from Depressionville to Angertown, to Uncertainsboro. Now you're in Risk City enjoying those perilous hairpin curves. Competence is right over the next mountain.

Be careful when you get to Competence. It's here that people often meet someone and merge on to the Love Turnpike, a well-maintained 8-lane expressway that goes right back to Depressionville.

Tip for the Day

If you see a biker wearing a t-shirt that reads, "Shit Happens," well, sir, you're looking at a fellow who's crying out for understanding.

Try saying to him, "There's truth to what your shirt says, my friend, but we still must take responsibility for our lives, for adversity. What you call 'shit' is really a lesson in strength!"

If he "happens" to kick the "shit" out of you, don't take it personally. He's really only angry at himself.

Passion

Have you ever seen one of those humongous chemical tankers coming down the highway, with a dinky little pick-up truck ahead of it that says "Danger, Wide Load"?

That's how most of us live our lives. We're all leading a big fat tanker full of precious, volatile feelings. *Passion*, I believe, is the chemical name, but we choose to drive the Fear truck instead, nursing the brakes, sticking to the safe route, making sure we don't spill any of those feelings.

Well, what good is a safe ride in a truck called Fear? Ditch it! Get behind the wheel of that Passion Tanker and let it rip, for if you can handle four tires, you can handle 18. Turn off for the side streets, and drop the hammer! Let no barricade stop you, no one-way sign discourage you. Turn the Johnny Cash music up full blast and head for Bourbon Street, Fifth Avenue, the *Champs-Elysées*, and Disneyland...Send the tourists sprawling! Life is meant to be a joyride, my friend. And should you come to a spectacular jack-knife finish, wheels up and steaming, know that its better to have spilled Passion everywhere than to have meekly followed Fear.

YOUR CAREER TIRE

"Problems are just opportunities in work clothes."
—STEEL MAGNATE HENRY KAISER

Quoted before dying of a misdiagnosed illness

YOUR CAREER THREE

Your Career Tire

The more overinflated your Career Tire, the more likely you are to go into a skid when it blows, and you're left unemployed. Your initial reaction will be panic. You'll try to wrest control of the situation. Don't!

The key is to go in the direction of your skid. In other words, go with the flow. Remember that when your Career Tire goes flat, you can still make a career out of managing your unemployment. No one tells you how to do it. YOU make the decisions. YOU put in as many hours as you want as a Self-Unemployed individual!

Occasionally, you might lose your resolve and start feeling worthless. If this happens, it's important to shift rejection away from yourself and toward others. Try calling up help-wanted numbers in the newspaper and turning them down on the spot:

> "Hello? I understand you're looking for a Waste Management Technician at $9.00 an hour? Well, thanks all the same, but I'm not interested. But, hang in there!"

Try it. Nothing inflates your sense of control more than saying "no!"

Now let's get to work on that Career Tire.

The Work Ethic & Gravy

The work ethic is not a substitute for love. You've heard of the expression "riding the gravy train."

There was a time when huge freight trains roamed this country, carrying gravy by the carload. People would wait at the station platforms with their wheelbarrows full of mashed potatoes, waiting for the Gravy Train to pull in. Some even jumped on to drink their fill right there! It was some sort of government program.

My grandfather was an engineer on one of those gravy trains. Every night, he would come home full of loathing and derision.

"I hate those gravy train riders," he would say. "Why, they're nothing but a bunch of good-for-nothing freeloaders!"

You know what was really bugging Grandpa? The fact that he worked hard while others got their share for free, then went home to spend time with their families.

Poor Grandpa never placed value on anything but hard work. He was a giving man, admittedly, most of it in gravy, but he could not *acknowledge* that he was a giving man. That old work ethic got in the way.

Grandpa's gone now. He died in a horrible giblet-car derailment. Sometimes I feel doomed to repeat his mistakes.

Tip for the Day

One of the cruelest signs is the one on the Greyhound Bus that says, "Do Not Talk to Driver While Bus Is in Motion." Believe me, that driver wants to talk, but his work ethic keeps him from showing any emotion.

It's up to you to break the ice. Say something like, "Boy, I'll bet you've driven through some real dumps."

Some Words of Inspiration

If you're searching for a career role model, you probably couldn't do better than the carnival worker.

The carnival worker has the perfect job. He takes
pride in keeping his Tilt-a-Whirl well oiled and spinning to
perfection. He sees the joy in every youngster's eyes—the
whirring, spinning, squeal-with-delight exhilaration of eternal childhood. And he knows the satisfaction of sitting back
at the end of the day and saying to himself, "At least I'm
not still in the slammer."

Tip for the Day

*Remember what I said earlier about the importance of
the word "I"?*

*There's a big difference between the words "I" and
"me." "I" implies power, as in "I am capable." "Me" is
passive, as in "Poor, poor pitiful me." "Me" is never at the
beginning of a sentence. Except, maybe, if you're a
Rastafarian.*

*It's important to start putting yourself at the top of
your sentences, my friend.*

*Practice walking around saying "I" over and over.
Say it loudly and vigorously, and every time you do you'll
feel another injection of confidence. It works!*

"I!"

*Do this at home and at work. If you feel self-conscious
yelling "I" in front of fellow employees, use the Spanish
translation, "Yo!" Everyone will think you're shouting at
them, but you're really making yourself feel damned good!*

Choosing a Career

Here's a little something I've learned from experience: People never lose their jobs because they can't do the work. They lose their jobs because they can't deal with people.

If you are consistently unhappy with most jobs you've had, then the very first question you need to ask yourself when choosing a career is, "How much can I stand to be around other people?"

This is a crucial question because a person's job happiness is directly proportional to how many people must be dealt with, which is why it's always disgruntled Post Office employees who shoot up the work place, never bee keepers.

Have a dream. Then set a goal. A dream is what you want to *be*. A goal is what you have to *reach* to be what you dream.

Example:

DREAM: To work at a job where I don't have to deal with people other than maybe touch their grubby hands.

GOAL: Toll booth operator on the Pennsylvania Turnpike.

See there? By following a dream *and* setting a goal, you choose a career.

Tip for the Day

You must project beyond your goals to your dream.

My big mistake was working too hard to make my House of Index Cards, Inc. profitable. I forgot all about my dream to be a respected and powerful pillar of the Office Supply Industry. I lost sight of my dream!

Probably the best way to keep sight of your dream is to tack it on to your first name. Like Famous Amos. Amos never forgot what he really wanted to be while he was baking those cookies. Evel Knievel is another example, except he never learned to spell.

Mile Markers

Reaching your goals will be easier if you devise a system of "Mile Markers."

Sit down with some 3 x 5 cards * and start listing all the things you need to achieve to reach your goal. Completing each one moves you another mile closer to your dream.

Let's say you're a woman who dreams of being a toll-booth attendant. Your list might look like this:

1. Drive to Pennsylvania. Pick most scenic exit.
2. Get job application.
3. Arrange interview. Present my "E-Z Flow" (5 cars FREE, 6th pays $20) plan to Turnpike Commissioner.
4. Acquire start-up change.
5. Begin training & preparation (stand in phone booth breathing noxious bus fumes).

Along with Mile Markers come the inevitable Road Hazard signs. Use your 3x5s to devise a contingency plan for dealing with these:

1. What if boyfriend objects to my new career? Plan: Dump Boyfriend

Tip for the Day

How come they call them "tollhouse" cookies? I've stopped at a lot of tollhouses but I never once got a cookie! If you're a tollbooth operator looking for incentives, fresh cookies would be a great way to pull more cars into your lane.

---

*Again, if you find that you've run short of index cards, we can work something out.

Money Isn't a Tree

When choosing a career, don't ruin it by agonizing over income.

When someone approaches me and asks what I earn per year, I know I'm talking to someone who will never truly understand wealth.

How often do we think of money as being something in trees? How many of us are *climbing* a *ladder of success*, working for *raises* and *promotions*, worrying about being *axed*, not happy until we're *pulling down* a couple hundred grand a year?

True wealth is in doing what you love, not in what you earn. It's a field, not a tree. I don't have to tell you most people are unhappy with their professions. A recent survey of 763 workers revealed 93% of them hated their jobs. The survey would have been more extensive but the pollster quit.

Tip for the Day

My Career Role Model is Mother Teresa. When I see the sheer number of lives she has touched, I'm almost envious. Boy, talk about clout and muscle. She's the Frank Sinatra of philanthropists!

A Mother Teresa project always gets the green light. When you've got the Pope and the Catholic Church bankrolling you, brother that's one sweet, sweet deal. She leaves all those other nuns in the dust!

The Five Locknuts for Securing Your Job

If you have chosen a career that involves interaction with other people, it is in your interest to get along with them, or else you'll just get canned again.

The Five Locknuts of Job Security are my patented five airwrench-tight techniques for allowing your customers, fellow employees and associates to walk away (or *drive* away if you're a tollbooth operator) feeling good about themselves and good about you. They are the locknuts that will keep your Career Tire bolted firmly in place.

Locknut #1: Know Your Limitations

I'm convinced the most honest product on America's store shelves is Milk Duds. Why? *Because it's willing to admit it's a failure.* It says so right on the box: Duds.

In fact, now and then, you'll come across a couple of Duds fused together, by accident. Somebody's letting *dud* Duds get through! If there's an exponential level of human error, this is it.

Yet, I can envision that moment in America's glorious, industrial past, when an intrepid supervisor stood before his army of chocolate workers, holding the pebbly lesions of chocolate in his nervous palm, and called out, "Gentlemen! We're actually gonna try to unload these things on the public. What shall we call them?"

He probably wasn't ready for the lusty candor of their replies:

"Lactic Failures!!"

"Dairy Mistakes!!"

"Cow Flops!!"

"Milk... Duds!!!!"

Of course, today we all know what resulted from that candor: one of America's all-time popular confections. Annual sales in the millions. And, most importantly, fierce loyalty to a product courageous enough to acknowledge its own shortcomings.

In a sense, we're all Lactic Failures. So why not just admit it? Tell your boss, your customers *and* yourself, "There's a really good chance I'm going to screw up." Ultimately, people will respond to your honesty.

Tip for the Day

If you can't get your books or receipts to balance out, here's a useful term vending machine distributors rely on: "Slug Factor."

Locknut #2: Compliment Everyone

You'd be amazed how many people find it hard to give out compliments. Everyone needs to be appreciated, yet we sometimes can't get the words out of our mouths. A little trick you might use is to lift blurbs from newspaper movie ads and apply them to people you work with. Tell someone they're "The feel-good employee of 1994!" If you like someone's proposal, tell them you "laughed, you cried, you cheered out loud!"

It's nice to give out raises and promotions, but sometimes a simple "Electrifying! ... an erotic sizzler, full of surprises ... Andy Garcia is *hot!*" will make someone feel 100% better about their job.

Tip for the Day

Everyone likes a compliment, but if someone says to you, "You're O.K. in my book!" this could very well mean they're writing a book—a book with a detailed list of who's "O.K." and who's "Not O.K.," perhaps with drawings and crude symbols and a satanic passage or two. Keep your distance.

Locknut #3: Never Forget a Name

Here's a little trick I use to remember people's names. Whenever I meet someone, I write their name down on an individually wrapped slice of cheese. This makes more of an impression than just pocketing their business card. I also make a small notation about that person on the cheese: hobbies, birthday, kid's names, whatever. (That really makes them feel special.) When I get home I file the cheese in a Rolodex. (Not by name, but by type of cheese; "C" for cheddar, etc.) Then, whenever I'm making a cheese sandwich I'll see the name and recall meeting that person. Once again, they'll be fresh in my memory.

If you've started your own business, make sure it has a snazzy name. A name may be the most important thing to set your goods or services apart from others, especially if what you have to offer is absolutely no different from your competitors.

A recent survey revealed that four out of five people who had their shirts One-Hour Martinized actually believed a guy named Martin personally tended to their soiled clothing. No one was clear on exactly what he did, but most believed him to be some sort of "dry cleaning genius."

A name means everything. Would you want your clothes to be "One-hour Floydinized"?

Tip for the Day

Remember, a worker never stands so tall as when he stoops to help a fellow employee. Especially if it's to pick up some severed fingers lost in a giant roller or something. And, if he were to run around smiling, with those fingers in a small can offering Vienna Sausages to workers, they'd know he was just a regular guy with a regular sense of humor.

Locknut #4: Remind Yourself
No Job Is Ever Too Small

Too many of us believe that our jobs are small and inconsequential. Well, there's no such thing, no sir!

Think of every skyscraper you've ever seen—an intricately laid assemblage of beams, supports and framework, each piece perfectly balanced. To achieve that balance, the builder relies on his carpenter's level. In the middle of the level sits a bubble swimming in yellow juice. Somewhere, there's a company that manufactures that juice. Do you know the name of that company? (If you said "Gatorade," you're wrong.)

Actually, I don't know the name of the company either. Yet, as I drive through my city each day, I'm glad someone cares enough about the quality of Yellow Leveling Juice to have never let a bad batch of it get through, because if they did, whoo-ee, there'd be gigantic skyscrapers falling all over the place!

Tip for the Day

Maybe it's just a penny gumball to you, but to the person who stocks the dispenser, each gumball is as unique and distinctive as a tiny chewable Faberge Egg, except instead of being worth $200,000, it's only worth about four cents. Though who can put a price on beauty and craftsmanship?

Locknut #5: Get Organized!

You will never effectively accomplish anything until you've learned to organize your time. This is the toughest Locknut of all. In fact, two of the most difficult topics I've mentioned in this book are: Organizing Your Time and Getting Rid of Fat. Both are nearly impossible. You know what might be easier? Organizing your fat!

Go down to your local meatcutter and ask him to weigh your various body parts. Using a large marker, outline each part and write the weight on it. If your thighs weigh 12 pounds apiece, write a big 12 on each thigh. By the time you're done you should loosely resemble that "Cuts of Meat" steer chart on the wall.

Now, look at yourself in the mirror and you'll see clearly what your "fat priorities" are.

Organizing your time is pretty much like organizing your fat. Figure out what weighs the most and tackle it first.

Tip for the Day!

Though organizing your time is important, organizing your things only creates suspicion. So stop worrying about cleaning your office! A clean desk indicates someone else is doing all the work. However, if you absolutely must clean your office, it'll go faster if you work clockwise. Pick a spot and mark it "twelve o'clock." Start cleaning in a clockwise direction. When you get to one o'clock, go to lunch.

Too Many Choices

Our lives are drowning in options! And it's eating up all our time. I like to watch T.V. as much as the next guy (five or six hours a night, tops) but nowadays it seems like it takes 15 minutes to go through all the 197 channels trying to decide what to watch. Well, that's 15 minutes *I* don't have to waste. It makes me mad.

Today's sad truth is we have become prisoners of "choice."

Did you ever wonder how the average prison inmate packs so much into one day? Well, maybe it's because he's *not* sitting around agonizing about what movie to see, what checkbook pattern, coffee maker, hair care product or Methodist Church to try. He's not lingering over the dessert cart at the prison mess. No sir! It's sheet cake or nothing because the man's got a job to do and *that's* why your license plates show up *on time* every year.

A prisoner doesn't *choose*. He *knows*. That's probably why he's called a "convict." By replacing your own "choices" with "convictions," you can save endless hours of time.

Tip for the Day

You could save everyone time and trouble if you settled on one color and model for everything in life.

Take Beige, Model 301 for example. I'll bet if you went down to the phone company and asked for a Beige Model 301, they'd have it. This also goes for appliances, catalog items, automobiles, insurance companies and bridesmaid's dresses—you name it.

There's way too much of everything! It doesn't matter if it's Beige Model 301 or Sea-Foam 1211 or Jumbo Camouflage, just pick one model and one color and stick with it! That way you'll know exactly what you want when you walk in the door..

What Causes Stress

We always think if we could just save time and trouble, we'd be less stressed. Wrong! Saving time and trouble doesn't cure stress, it causes stress.

Postal workers are the perfect example. We've done everything we can to make the job easier. We've put little numbers on our houses. It's not like they have to stand in the middle of the street yelling, "Johnson!! Where's Johnson!! Come out here and get your mail!!!!" We've bought them little jeeps and shorts and pith helmets. What more do they want? *Why* are they shooting at everyone?

Because the more time and trouble we save, the more stressed we get.

We've become time-saving addicts! We want hyper-access and nano-second responses. (Take a look at which companies are profitable right now! Fed-Ex, U.P.S. and Domino's. Look who's losing their shirts: G.M., Sears and I.B.M. We're making lots of crappy stuff and delivering it really fast!)

Once fixated on eliminating time and trouble, some of us graduate to the next level—eliminating humans. (The *source* of most of our time and trouble.)

Thus, you have to understand the average disgruntled postal employee wielding a semi-automatic rifle has ultimately adopted a more minimalist approach to his livelihood. He's cutting through the paperwork!

Tip for the Day

Stress always leads to accident or error. An accident is getting your tie caught in moving machinery. An error is making the wrong keyboard input and wiping out the Mormon Church's financial holdings.

You can usually recover from an accident, but nobody wants a pack of Mormon Elders birddogging for them.

If you make an error, keep quiet. If you have an accident, make as much noise as you can. There's money in it.

Eliminate Things That Beep

We've been shortchanged by science! All the sci-fi movies and television programs of the past led us to believe the present day would be full of soothing sounds, of doors and panels that went "whoosh," landing gears that "whirred" and ultra-convenient gadgets that "trilled." It was a comforting cacophony of future living.

So what did we get? Beeping!

Our days are now a relentless pealing of beeping phones demanding to be answered, beeping pocket pagers reeling off urgent messages, beeping watches reminding us we're late, beeping trucks threatening to back over us, computers, smoke detectors, alarms, microwave ovens...beep, beep, beep, beeeeeeep....!

Maybe beep-beeping is burning *you* out. Remember, beeping only signifies urgency or malfunction and who needs *that*? Eliminate things that beep, and you can say goodbye to most of the stress in your life.

One needs only to look at Wile E. Coyote to see that cartoons are more prescient than scientific research. Brilliant pyrotechnician that he was, Wile E. sadly allowed beep-beeping to make his life an unmanageable, disheveled mess.

Tip for the Day

WHAT IF?

I always trained my employees to never use those words, "What if we run out of stock?" "What if we get robbed?" "What if we get hurt on the job? Are we covered?"

Worrying about "what if" means you're stuck in the future, trying to control the unknown.

I always made my employees deal in the here and now. They never walked around saying "what if?" They walked around saying, "What's going on?" Big difference.

Fear & Stress

Here's how the Holmes-Rahe Life Events Scale rates the following activities (note the ones I've circled):

Event	Stress Units
Death of Spouse	100
Divorce	73
Marital Separation	65
Jail Term	63
Death of Close Family Member	63
Personal Injury or Illness	53
Marriage	50
Fired at Work	47
Marital Reconciliation	45
Retirement	45
Change in Health of Family Member	44
Pregnancy	40
Gain New Family Member	39
Sex Difficulties	39
Business Readjustment	39
Change in Financial State	38
Death of Close Friend	37
Change to Different Line of Work	36
Change in Number of Arguments with Spouse	35
High Mortgage	31
Foreclosure of Mortgage or Loan	30
Change in Responsibilites at Work	29
Son or Daughter Leaving Home	29
Trouble with In-Laws	29
Outstanding Personal Achievement	28
Begin or End School	26
Change in Living Conditions	25
Revision of Personal Habits	24

Trouble with Boss	*23*
Change in Hours or Conditions at Work	*20*
Change in Residence	*20*
Change in Schools	*20*
Change in Church Activities	*19*
Change in Recreation	*19*
Change in Social Activities	*18*
Small Mortgage or Loan	*17*
Change in Sleeping Habits	*16*
Change in Number of Family Get-Togethers	*15*
Change in Eating Habits	*15*
Vacation	*13*
Christmas	*12*
Minor Violations of the Law	*11*

I think this shows you how misguided our perception can be. A shaky guy at a nuclear plant who just got reamed by his boss is only a 23, but a couple barrelling down the highway pulling a mobile home with "Just Married" written on its windows rates a combined total of 108. They're off the scale!

Boy, I wish I had this chart the night of my House of Index Cards Grand Opening. Look at what I was batting:

BUSINESS READJUSTMENT	*39*
CHANGE IN FINANCIAL STATE	*38*
CHANGE TO DIFFERENT	
LINE OF WORK	*36*
CHANGE IN LIVING CONDITIONS	*25*
(Persuading Gretel to move to the Tubman Shelter)	
SMALL MORTGAGE OR LOAN	*17*
CHRISTMAS	*12*
SEX DIFFICULTIES	*39*
(Fighting with my girlfriend, OKAY?)	___
TOTAL	*206*

Man, that's beyond stress. That's fission. I suppose if I hadn't kicked my Aunt Gretel out, if my girlfriend had used the few precious hours we spent together to be more accommodating instead of weeping uncontrollably *and* if I had waited 'til after Christmas to open, I would have been thinking more clearly and probably would have not made the inept decision to locate the House of Index Cards in the middle of the mall Food Court. So it goes.

Get your personal life together before you launch a business!

Tip for the Day

Three most important words in Real Estate: Location! Location! Location!

Three most important words in Business: Specialize! Specialize! Specialize!

Three most important words in opening an Index Card Store in a Food Court: Lost Our Lease!

Just a joke. Good thing I can laugh at a tragic situation, huh?

Every Product Has a Soul

Every product has a soul, a consciousness, that comes from its maker. I always stressed to each and every customer who walked into my House of Index Cards that I was not merely selling them a stack of index cards, but rather an entity through which they might collect, organize and expand their own thoughts. Of course, I was usually explaining this to some slack-jawed mall rat holding a cup of curly fries and wondering where the video arcade was. Sometimes the product has more of a consciousness than the customer.

Tip for the Day

A TRUE SALESMAN NEVER GIVES UP

It does no good when a potential customer is exiting your establishment empty-handed to offer some trite pleasantry to him. Nobody ever turned around and bought something because you called out, "Thanks for coming in!" or "Have a nice day."

When a customer is walking out the door, it's time to muster one last effort and shout out something like, "You're making one hell of a big mistake not buying anything!" or "Why did you come in here, to <u>tease</u> me?"

Inspiration: An Anecdote

Some people might say the reason my House of Index Cards, Inc. failed was because it was a bad idea. But I say THERE'S NO SUCH THING!

You know what inspiration is? Why it's nothing more than a recycled bad idea.

I was told that the Ferris Wheel was originally designed as a form of public transportation. That's right, John Compton Ferris' dream was to construct a gigantic wheel that would carry passengers from St. Louis to Kansas City, Missouri and back. He envisioned the day the wheels would crisscross the country carrying two, three, four hundred people at a time between its spokes. Some of them would even have lounge cars!

But, on its maiden voyage in 1895, the Ferris Wheel proved a disaster, wobbling off course and crushing everything and everyone in its path.

One man who wasn't crushed, however, was Ferris. He kept thinking and rethinking the idea until bingo! It occurred to him to make the wheel *stationary*.

So, if you have ideas that are "going nowhere," look closer. Maybe they're supposed to!

Tip for the Day

Study all the world's truly great success or motivational classics—"*How to Win Friends and Influence People*," "*What Color is Your Parachute?*" and "*The Autobiography of Attila the Hun*"—and you will soon notice they all say the same thing: a great success or motivational book needs lots of anecdotes.

Anecdotes are quite powerful for they are hearty examples of <u>doing</u>. The best ones are written in prison, where they are honed to mythic levels of inspiration and then passed on to the high echelons of leadership. Use them often!

Perseverance: An Anecdote

Good ideas are a dime a dozen. But it's the persistent ones that get implemented. Taking my own advice, here's an anecdote on perseverance.

Earlier this century, the Treasury Department held a huge meeting to redesign the dollar bill. There were dozens of suggestions for what symbols might best reflect America's heritage.

"An eagle," someone shouted.

"Good idea!" everyone murmured.

"A flag!"

"A tall ship with masts!"

"Lady Liberty!"

"Pilgrims!"

"Indians!"

But from the back of the room there was one voice that kept calling out, "How about a pyramid sort of thing with a giant eyeball on top?" And you only need to look at the back of any dollar bill today to see how that perseverance paid off.

Tip for the Day

People are kind of like car batteries. Batteries have a "positive" terminal and a "negative" terminal. The positive terminal is "alive" and full of "juice." Sometimes they both collect some kind of greenish-white crusty stuff that makes us think to ourselves, "If I ate that crusty stuff, I bet I'd die." I never said it was a great metaphor.

YOUR SPIRITUALITY TIRE

"Barry Longo is the master of the Western mind."
—from an advertisment in *Body and Mind Magazine* for "A Course in *Being,* with Barry Longo" which, upon attending, turned out to be more like "A Course in *being with* Barry Longo"

A Word About Your Spirituality Tire

Many people who attend my Self-Help for the Bleak seminars voice the same complaint, "Why do I feel so empty inside?" I always answer their question with another question, a profoundly simple one, "What makes a tire a tire?"

They usually stare at me quizzically, and I have to repeat the question.

"What makes a tire a tire?"

"I don't know," they reply. "Rubber. Steel Belts. Vulcanizing. What does that have to do with the donkey ride to hell my life has become?"

"A tire is a tire by its roundness," I tell them calmly. "And what makes it round is its center. Yet, there is no center to a tire, is there? Why, there's nothing. A hole. Emptiness. But that tire was built on a form and the form is what gave it its roundness. That form is called Spirituality. Just because we cannot see Spirituality doesn't mean it doesn't exist.

"A tire only stays flat when an earthly vehicle sits on it. When you remove the pressure of that earthly vehicle, the tire regains its roundness. The tire is reshaped by its spirituality.

"Thus, in order to be truly spiritual we must remove our tires from our earthly vehicle. Then they will regain their roundness. The center will still be invisible, but it will be invisible of Spirituality, not Emptiness."

I like to think it's answers like these—secular explanations to metaphysical questions—that make my seminars so effective.

Icons of Serenity

Don't go overboard with your spirituality. A few out-ward trappings are all you need to convey your "special" Inner Knowledge and Serenity.

If you were to make a pilgrimage to the East to find the original Book of Tao and held it in your hands—its pages yellowed from the centuries—you could look inside and likely find some big answers to Life. But those answers would be very cryptic—lots of stuff about Lao-Tzu and the "essence of female balance." Also, the book's probably in a museum, so there'd be no time to really read it, because, hey, the staff wants to go home.

It's much easier just to zip over to New Mexico and hold the Book of Taos in your hands. Its pages, too, will be yellow. And inside you'll find a lot of listings for Mexican restaurants, art galleries and cowpoke furniture stores. When you get back home and friends see your ceremonial Navajo porch chimes and faux-oxidized candle holders, hoo-boy they'll *know* you're really "centered."

Tip for the Day

Don't confuse "spiritual" with "religious." Religion is the road that spirituality travels on.

All religions ultimately lead to the truth. Some are gigantic interstates, others narrow, winding one-lanes. Of course, no one ever arrives at the truth until they're dead. So, whenever I'm driving and I pass a funeral motorcade, I never feel sad for the person in the hearse. I rejoice for them, knowing they're about to find the Truth. Then I hang a U-ee and join the procession. Hell, I was headed the wrong way!

Simplicity: An Anecdote

There's a story the oldtimers of Niagara Falls love to tell about how the great bridge across the Falls first began. A kite was flown above the Falls. Attached to the kite was a string. Attached to the string was a rope. Attached to the rope was steel cable. And from that cable workers were ultimately able to suspend one of the most spectacular bridges of modern times.

I never fail to get a kick out of hearing the crusty denizens of Niagara Falls retell this story. It seems a classic illustration of how all great accomplishments begin with a simple childlike endeavor.

But then the more I think about it, the more I realize great achievements don't begin with childlike ideas at all, but rather with confusion and ineptness and a lot of people running around with no clue whatsoever about what they're supposed to be doing (but they're in a union so who cares?). Eventually the project gets completed, but way over budget, and besides, what kind of moron brings a kite to work anyway?

This is a classic example of how an inspirational story starts out about something like "simplicity" and ends up being about a bunch of old coots hanging around a tourist trap spinning the same tired yarn.

Tip for the Day

Always take the road less traveled. Unless it's through Gallup, New Mexico. Man, I wouldn't get out of the car there even if I was Charles Kuralt.

The Spirituality of Bad Credit

Credit is like a drug. When you can't get it anymore you sober up fast and start to see with real clarity.

As the material things in my life disappeared (or were repossessed) I actually began to feel freer in spirit. Unencumbered, so to speak. I was able to float above my financial situation and look down on it. It was what I call an "Out of Money Experience." I saw many debts and unpaid bills both past and present. My Chapter 11 filing floated into view and I was able to see checks stamped "Returned Due To Insufficient Funds."

The Out of Money Experience is a passive, spiritual act, and especially bleak. (Being out of money and feeling bleak just seem to go together.) See, our entire system of life is defined by money and material success. Subvert that system by not having either and you'll destroy everything the system holds dear.

Inevitably, your Experience will be acknowledged by a Higher Financial Power, such as the I.R.S., the Mafia or some loan sharks, which could lead to other spiritual experiences. Like an Out of Body Experience—if they happen to shoot you.

Tip for the Day

Money is the arch-enemy of creativity! It makes us lazy and inhibits our ingenuity.

A true artist knows his reward is in the muse, not the paycheck, and the very act of trying to accomplish something with little or no money is the most rewarding artistic process of all.

Of course, you'd have a hard time convincing folks in Appalachia they're living in an artist's colony.

How to Get Out of Debt

Debt is imprisonment. It's that simple. As a prison controls its inmates by restricting their freedom of movement, our creditors control us. Of course, we try to fight them. Feeble gesture!

The only way to escape debt is to surrender and give yourself up! Say to your creditors, "You got me. I'm your prisoner."

Now, as a prisoner, you get to ask permission for every move you make. Feel free to call up the banks and credit card companies two or three hundred times a day. Pretend you're one of those Georgia Work Farm inmates and use a lyrical "prison" cadence:

> "Permission to get a haircut today, Big Bank Boss?"
> "Can I get a second helping of dessert, Master Card?"
> "Been draggin' the line double-time, Credit Man. Can I have a drink of water?"

Pretty soon they'll stop taking your calls. Show up in person. Stand in the middle of the bank lobby, unbuttoning your shirt and shouting, "Takin' it off today, boss!"

Soon enough they'll lock the doors when they see you coming. *Now* who's the prisoner? You win!

Tip for the Day

Things are never so overwhelming when you learn to live one day at a time. Occasionally it's a good idea to write up your obituary and print it in the paper. List your accomplishments. Where you came from. Who you loved. Who survived you.

An obituary really defines your life. It lets you and others truly appreciate what you've done in the little squirt of time you've spent on the planet. And, it entitles you to be "reborn" and begin your life anew.

Also, be sure to send copies of the obit to all the people you owe money to. Maybe they'll stop bugging you.

What the New Age Means to You

So many people today are pausing to take a look around and see if there might be more to life than just career and consumption. Without question, we have emerged into an era of self-enlightenment—call it the New Age if you must—but for the first time there appears the possibility of a global harmonium of humans who place a higher value on self-awareness and healing than on careers and money.

What does this mean to you? Profit, that's what! The pathway to higher self-consciousness is a long, arduous one. People are going to want to pick up some souvenirs along the way. These "ethereal bodies" have hard cash and they're snapping up every gloopy memento they can get their hands on. Don't lose out! Get in there and pitch your concession tent before the New Age passes you by.

Like my Aunt Gretel used to say, "When life hands you lemmings, make lemmingade!"

Tip for the Day

A good title for a subliminal self-help tape would be "Head Cleaner." I bet you'd sell a bunch just by accident.

THE PATHWAY TO HIGHER SELF-CONSCIOUSNESS IS A LONG,
ARDUOUS ONE. PEOPLE ARE GOING TO WANT TO PICK UP SOME
SOUVENIRS ALONG THE WAY.

Savoring Life

To watch a child is to know what it means to be "living in the moment." Ever see a child enthralled with a bug? The child will spend hours studying the bug, oblivious to everything else around him. Nothing present or past matters, just the movements of that bug.

We could learn a lot from that child. But we could learn more from the bug, which, with that big eyeball staring down at him, knows his life is as cheap as a child's whimsical decision to crush him.

Though the child is living "in the moment," the bug is living "only for a moment."

In a sense, we are all living only for a moment. So scurry and try to look busy, my friend, for God has a short attention span and is just waiting to grind you to pieces with one satisfying crunch of his heel.

Tip for the Day

Keep a diary of imaginative, completely fictional details. It's a great creative outlet and, should an untimely death befall you, folks will read it and you'll become a posthumous legend! Sample Entries:

Sun. April 9

Aquahol experiments an astounding success! 700 m.p.g! Tap water no problem.

Fri. June 10

Tapes sound phenomenal! Ringo's drumming never better. Paul begs me to teach him my slide technique. George—pensive, as always.

Your Special Place

Your inner child has always been there. It's that part of you that needs to "play," to be released from the harsh responsibility of adulthood. Unfortunately, society does not yet allow us to release this inner child at random. You can't exactly stop a board of directors' meeting and blurt out, "Hey everyone, let's build a fort!"

Thus, we all need to find a "special place." As a kid, we all had a "special place," a place that was ours alone, where we could romp and play and let our imaginations run wild—where anything was possible.

Find your own special place. Tell yourself, "This is where I will come from now on to unleash my inner child. This will be my magical place." My own preference is Caesar's Palace in Vegas, but that's just me. You may prefer a more spiritual environment, like Circus Circus or Bob Stupaks' Vegas World.

Tip for the Day

Your inner child is not a psychological conceit. Your inner child is real. You simply have to find it. The easiest way is to have it paged at Sears. Go to the Service Desk and have them announce over the loudspeaker, "We have a lost inner child at the Service Desk named (your name). Will the owner please claim it?" Hearing your inner child announced loudly over the P.A. will melt the barriers you've spent years erecting between the two of you. Once you've reunited, go visit the toy department. You won't believe the cool stuff they have nowadays.

Ego

Never forget that everyone, no matter how humble they seem, has an ego.

Let's say you're driving through India with the Maharishi Yogi, basking in the illumination of his presence, totally at peace with the world. Suddenly, a bee flies in the window and, next thing you know, the Maharishi is flailing around like some kind of spazzo marionette, swatting at the bee with a rolled-up copy of unpublished mantras.

Sure, you'd both have a good laugh. He might even reach over and kiss you on the cheek to acknowledge such a funny "human" moment. But it would be the kiss of death, brother, because his whole "worlds' calmest guy" rep has just been shot. You've seen too much. You're a dead man.

Tip for the Day

If you do decide to get in touch with your inner child, you'd better be ready to go the distance, because if you only try half-heartedly you're gonna get stuck with your "man-teen," a fifteen-year-old grunge rocker trapped in drivers' license limbo who nobody understands.

Spiritual Resource Material

"Instead of imbibing spirits," my friend suggested, "why don't we try imbibing some spirituality?" I was reluctant, but I decided to give it a try. So we forewent our usual Sunday afternoon get-together at the Likker Locker and instead went to the Bodhi Tree, Southern California's most enlightened bookstore. Boy did I feel uneasy pulling up to it. I asked myself why.

"Why do I *fear* spirituality?" Because, I decided, it is the furthermost tire from my driving seat, the one I am least in touch with.

But just as important, I reminded myself. When I saw how many self-help/new-age/metaphysical books there were I was pretty astounded. About the only thing I can tell you is when you blow a spiritual tire, there's always another one in stock. Your Spiritual Tire is a 16-inch standard radial, and that's good news.

But, what I was really amazed to see was that *everywhere you looked new age guys were hitting on new age women*! *And vice versa.* Every incense-fogged corner of the store was taken up by someone matching their aromatherapy chart with someone else's, "fennelizing" or whatever, fetching red zingers for their prospective pickups, reading each other's chakras, talking that "nurturing" jive. The place was hopping!

I learned a valuable spiritual lesson that day: A new-age bookstore is a great place for cruising. And no cover!

Tip for the Day

It's time corporations started developing a collective consciousness. Let me give you an example:

I'll bet "Crips" and "Bloods" never copyrighted those names. If some company started marketing "Crispy Crip Cereal," gang members would probably start to feel cheap and commercialized. Or how about "Bloods Troll Dolls"? Once they saw what corporate America was doing to their image (and their hair), that's it, the whole gang thing would just fall apart.

Co-Dependent Planet

My five-year-old niece, Krista, and I were horseback riding one night and she asked me if there was really a "man" in the moon. "Sure there is, Krista," I replied. "But he has really low self-esteem. He gravitates toward the Earth because he believes a 'quality' planet like Mercury or Saturn wouldn't have anything to do with him. So he hangs around a 'loser' like Earth, even though Earth walked all over him and now pretty much ignores him.

"But, one of these days that old man in the moon is gonna get fed up with Earth's rampant self-abuse. He's gonna pack up and leave. When he does, the tides will get screwy and we'll all drown. Earth really needs the moon, she just won't admit it."

Boy, that gave her something to chew on for the rest of the trip.

Tip for the Day

I'm not sure why the New Age movement is so big, but I think it has something to do with the disappearance of families. People just want to be part of something, especially if it embraces them unconditionally, which the New Age movement does. Shamans, whales and spiritual guides are just substitute relatives; and the cryptic insights people seek through channeling, theta consciousness, and colon rejuvenation aren't really much different than sitting around hearing your Aunt Gretel dispense some addled bromide, like "Don't get stuck between a hard rock and a cafe."

So before you go off and blow 500 bucks to spend the weekend contacting your personal goddess through "telepathic empowerment," stop for a moment to consider that maybe you have a cousin in Nebraska you haven't called lately.

Becoming One with Chad

Each and every one of us feels the need to be more in touch with the planet. "Listen to the planet," we're told, "for it will tell us what it needs." But the problem is, the planet is so damned big, there are probably parts of it we can't ever hear. Lesotho, for example.

It might be easier to try and get in touch with one particular part of the planet...a single country for example.

I believe each of us has our own personal country, a country whose culture and conflicts parallel our own. There are passive countries and aggressive countries, shy countries and outgoing countries. Some, like the U.S. and Australia, are male. They are very domineering and not too in touch with themselves. Other countries, like India or Peru, are more rooted in the Earth, and thus female. They're the ones getting walked all over. Canada is asexual.

To find your country, consult an almanac until you've found the nation that's persona is closest to your own. This requires a bit of intuition but you'll know it when you find it. Perhaps you're an industrious person whose efforts go largely unnoticed. You're a Qatar. If your life is pretty much a vast wasteland, you're a Greenland. Once you've determined your country, scan the newspaper as you would an astrology chart. Look for bits of news that can help determine the course of your own development. For instance, if you're an Italy and a series of bombs goes off in Rome, it could mean it's time to diversify your stock portfolio.

Tip for the Day

Incidentally, in case you're wondering, I'm a Nepal. I arrived at this when I noticed Nepal is landlocked. I hate the ocean. Nepal is fifteen minutes out of synch with the World Clock; I'm chronically late for everything. The capital of Nepal is Katmandu; I'm a huge Ted Nugent fan. Thus, I am in harmony with Nepal.

Everyone Is Looking for Direction

If someone in a car stops to ask you for directions, never say, "I don't know" or "You can't get there from here." The place they are looking for could be the culmination of their dream, the pot at the end of the rainbow. Do *you* want to be the person who bursts their fragile bubble? God knows, they've probably had enough setbacks already. Give them directions, *any* directions. Even if you have to lie! Tell them to go straight for 3 miles where your brother will meet them and lead them in. Give them the will to keep going! They need it.

Tip for the Day

You don't have to believe in God to be spiritual. You simply have to be overwhelmed by life. It's kind of like hearing "oh, boy!" during sex, instead of "oh, God!" It's almost the same.

Man's Wounded Warrior Spirit

Woman and man once hunted and gathered together in harmony. But with the development of agriculture, that harmony crumbled. Marauders began trying to steal the crops, so Peaceful Man took to arming himself in defense. He became a Warrior.

The "Wounded Warrior Spirit" still exists in man today. He would like to go back to peaceful hunting and gathering, but he can't bring himself to do it. He enjoys chasing marauders too much.

Which is why modern man is reluctant to go shopping. To a man, shopping is an evolved form of hunting and gathering, and his wounded warrior spirit can't deal with that.

If you really want your husband or boyfriend to go shopping with you, tell him he can chase all the shoplifters. Then he'll be enthusiastic.

Tip for the Day

My Aunt Gretel says:

If you're going shopping for groceries, always eat a big meal before. That way you'll buy less.

If you're going shoplifting, don't eat anything. You'll have more room to stuff items down your pants.

Respect for Individuality

Next time you're introduced to someone at a party or get-together and the first thing they ask you is, "What do you do?" don't be so quick to tell them. Try saying something like:

"What you are really asking me is, 'What do I do to make money?' If I told you, you would immediately classify me according to your preconceived, arbitrary notions of that particular occupation. No my friend, I cannot allow you to put a handle on me without regard to my true personal feelings and opinions, for that would jeopardize my individuality."

More than likely the person will say, "What a fruitbat," and walk away. What the hell, they weren't worth knowing in the first place.

Tip for the Day

Another way to avoid this question is to ask it first. Asking "What do I do?" to someone you've just met gives an interesting dynamic to the encounter. They'll probably lead you around, introduce you to lots of folks, get you some snacks and ditch you.

A Sense of Belonging

Alienation is a horribly bleak feeling.

You'll always be alienated until you can master the knack of Belonging to the Right Now.

Next time you're walking down the road and find a quarter, don't just pick it up and think, "Hey, I found this quarter. Now it belongs to me." Instead, say, "I found this quarter and now *I* belong to *it*." Lie down with the quarter. Eventually, someone else will come along and find both a new quarter and a new friend.

When you accept that you are part of the things and people of the moment, you will truly understand what belonging is.

You might think it was "colorful" if a waiter in a diner in Queens was holding up someone's overlooked coat and yelling, "Hey, who's left a jacket! Who belongs to dis thing, huh?" but I believe that waiter possesses a depth of spirituality most of us could only hope to reach.

Tip for the Day

The brain is just a radio. When it breaks down, we can no longer hear the music. But that doesn't mean the music's not still there. It's just on a higher frequency. The crazy guy we see shuffling down the street screaming, "Don't tell me I can't cross the 38th parallel, you punk! I finished my pancakes!" is simply listening to a different frequency—talk radio probably.

Only Human

No matter how much we strive for perfection, we cannot truly reach it. In every handmade Navajo rug there is a small bit of stitching that does not follow the pattern. It is an unavoidable imperfection and weavers call it a "Christian error." The Christian error is there to remind us we're only human.

You've probably heard of the Chunnel, England and France's joint underwater link project. In 1986, two teams of drillers, one English and one French, started at respective ends of the English Channel. They drilled around-the-clock at an absolutely exhaustive pace and still fell far behind schedule. Finally, in February of 1992, the two teams "punched through." And guess what I heard? They were off by two feet! All the intensive calculations in the world could not account for the fact that the teams missed each other.

Pretty soon the 48 mile tunnel will be open for traffic. When the chunnel train reaches the middle, it will have to "make a quick little jog to the right." There could be a few spectacular derailments. Oh well, "Christian error."

Tip for the Day

"It's the journey, not the destination."

Perhaps the single most important piece of advice ever imparted are those simple words. But don't forget sometimes it's a weird destination, like when someone has a near-death experience and travels through that tunnel with the blinding white light at the end and there's an angel with her arms outstretched. I don't need to tell you, it's the person who bounces through that tunnel whooping and turning somersaults and singing, "Ahooooooo! Werewolves of London..." who truly understands the meaning of, "It's the journey, not the destination."

A FINAL
WORD

A Final Word

I foolishly asked my tire repairman, as he was fixing yet another leak in my tire, why no one had invented a 'flat-proof' tire, made of Nerf or something. I guess he must get that question a lot because his answer was a little too pat.

"Tires are rubber. Rubber is petroleum. Petroleum is O.P.E.C. A 'flat-proof' tire would upset the delicate Middle East balance and ultimately lead to Armageddon. Also, it would bounce all over the place."

Sort of the same can be said for Self-Help books. C'mon, you didn't really expect a cheap $9.95 paperback to fix anything, did you? But they're great for pumping airy self-intent into your system. When you're dancing through life like a chicken on a hot-plate, who's got time for intro-spection?

As a flat-proof tire is merely an ideal, so is true happi-ness and well-being. Our tires *have* to blow out occasionally, for only in crisis do we truly awaken to our surroundings and grow. A car on four solid tires would end up bouncing all over the place. So would a society of happy, well-adjusted people. (If you've ever seen *Up With People*, you know what I'm talking about.)

If you're depressed, try to find a book that will at least elevate you to "miserable." If you're miserable, try to get unhappy. If you're unhappy, be happy you're unhappy. It keeps the economy rolling!

About the Author

As a stand-up performer, Rich Hall has appeared in major clubs and theaters throughout the United States and England. He was an Emmy award–winning writer for *Late Night With David Letterman* and a performer on *Saturday Night Live* and HBO's *Not Necessarily the News*. His humor series *Sniglets* became a best-seller, and *Onion World* is his critically acclaimed TV show featured on Comedy Central. Rich resides in the northern Rockies.